CHRISTIANITY IN THE WORKPLACE: YOUR FAITH ON THE JOB

LAY ACTION MINISTRY PROGRAM
5827 S. RAPP ST.
LITTLETON, CO 80120

DAVID C. COOK PUBLISHING CO.
850 N. GROVE AVE.
ELGIN, IL 60120

David C. Cook Publishing Co.
850 North Grove Avenue
Elgin, IL 60120
Printed in U.S.A.

Editor: Gary Wilde
Designer: Chris Patchel
Cover: Lois Rosio Sprague

ISBN: 0-89191-487-0
Library of Congress Catalog Number: 89-60267

TABLE OF CONTENTS

PREFACE

"There is a lot more to being a Christian in business than just responding to ethical issues." We made this point to Bob Samms, Executive Director of Lay Action Ministry Program (LAMP), during a breakfast meeting a few months ago. Bob had been teaching a Sunday School class on ethics in business and the workplace.

We pointed out that the key issues in business include gaining competitive advantage, achieving excellence, and seeking personal and corporate renewal. These subjects have been popularized in recent books by Michael Porter of the Harvard Business School, *Competitive Advantage*, *Competitive Strategies;* by Bob Waterman and Tom Peters, *In Search of Excellence;* and by Waterman, *The Renewal Factor.*

After a long discussion of the various issues and opportunities facing a Christian at work, Bob responded with a challenge: Why don't we write a book for lay people on the subject of Christianity in the business world? The book would be used to stimulate discussion in small groups, Bible studies, or Sunday school classes.

Following development of an outline of subjects to be covered (see the table of contents), it became obvious to us that we lacked the "real world" experience to write intelligently about all 12 subjects. So we decided to use a focus group approach.

Focus group interviews are a popular and useful market research technique. In most focus groups, a dozen or so persons gather in a conference room to discuss a particular subject, often a new product or service, for about two hours. The discussion is led by a moderator who works from a checklist of questions. Thus, the discussions are "focused" on a market research issue. The discussions are tape-recorded (sometimes with videotape) and analyzed to form the basis for decision making.

LAMP Focus Group Participants

In this case we selected 13 persons, all of them employed, and asked them to meet with us weekly for a 12-week period. Each session lasted an hour and a half. We refer to our participants' responses throughout the book, using their first names. We extend our gratitude and thanks to each of them. (For present-day mini-cases, even first names have been changed.)

For the discussion of the special challenges that unfold when both husband and wife work, we invited three additional working women. For the session on losing a job and being unemployed, we invited three additional men, and on the issue of doing business with other Christians, we also included four more guests.

We hope this book will provide the basis for stimulating discussion and for renewing commitments in dealing with the issues and opportunities afforded Christians in the workplace.

Note on Dual Authorship

To avoid awkwardness of speech, "we" is used throughout the book to refer to both authors. "I" is used when one of the authors refers to himself exclusively.

—Dean Coddington and Donald Orvis

LAY ACTION MINISTRY PROGRAM

LAMP Courses are based on the HEAD, HEART, and HANDS approach to learning. HEAD represents Bible *content* that you want to know. HEART represents your *personal application* of the truth. HANDS refers to the LAMP goal of preparing you to *use course content in the lives of other people*—imparting to others what you have learned (see II Tim. 2:2).

Christianity in the Workplace can be a life-changing study experience. If you diligently study each lesson, this course can transform your understanding of ministry, help you understand your ministry gifts, and encourage you to launch into a ministry for Christ.

How to Use This Course

This course is for every Christian who is willing to put forth the effort in personal study. But we want you to know "up front" what it is going to cost you in terms of time and commitment. *It is going to cost you a good hour of home study for each lesson.* Make every effort to spend this much time as a minimum requirement.

Though you may complete the course by yourself, you will normally be preparing for a weekly group meeting. In this meeting you will be an active participant because of your personal study. One lesson is to be completed each week, prior to coming to the weekly group meeting.

The weekly group meeting for this course features a discussion of the lesson that you have studied during the week. It also includes other elements to encourage group life, and to guide group members toward personal application of the material. The meeting, planned for at least a full hour, should be led by a person who enjoys leading discussions and helping people learn. The leader will study the lesson in the same way as anyone else in the group with the aid of the four-step lesson plans at the back of this book. In addition, an extended **Leader's Guide** is available that provides specific suggestions for conducting each weekly group meeting. This **Leader's Guide** can be obtained from:

LAY ACTION MINISTRY PROGRAM, INC.
5827 SOUTH RAPP STREET
LITTLETON, CO 80120

or:
DAVID C. COOK PUBLISHING CO.
850 NORTH GROVE AVENUE
ELGIN, IL 60120

1

LIFE'S PRIORITIES

The young CPA sat across from me in his office. He was talking about his future with the large international public accounting firm he had been with for the past four years. "Every time you get promoted, they expect more hours of your time. I'm a manager now, and I put in 50 to 60 hours a week. When I get to be a partner, the firm will expect 60 to 70 hours." He went on to say, "I've got two small children, and I want to spend more time with them and my wife. We are active in our church and I like to play golf on occasion, too." His eventual decision: give up a promising corporate career and go into business for himself.

Did this young professional make the right decision? What if he finds it difficult to establish his own practice, and his family's finances suffer? And what if he finds that being in charge of a small business takes more time and energy than he anticipates? Are we Christians to take the less demanding jobs—for the sake of our families—and let others take the really tough ones, those that pay more?

Having been around a few more years than this young CPA, I can appreciate his dilemma. The book, *Celebration of Discipline, the Path to Spiritual Growth* by Richard J. Foster (1978, Harper & Row) tells us that a Christian should spend time meditating, studying the Bible, praying, worshiping, and practicing several other disciplines. As active laymen and church members, we are involved in such activities as: singing in the choir, meeting in small group Bible studies, attending Sunday school and Sunday morning worship, and often participating in special fund-raising, strategic planning, or other short-term committee assignments.

Our doctors tell us that we need to exercise regularly—at least a brisk hour-long walk several times a week in addition to playing squash or racquetball regularly. Our wives and families like to see us, too.

Then there are our businesses. We have a responsibility to pay employees' salaries, keep them busy, and provide opportunities for their professional growth. Business travel takes time—usually two or three short trips per month. Then there are Rotary Club and hospital board meetings, plus other civic and professional activities.

We chose to begin *Christianity in the Workplace* with a discussion of the problem of setting (and living) appropriate priorities. We will refer extensively to the comments and reactions of a "focus group" in this chapter and others—a group of people who were questioned about their experiences in the workplace and how they relate their work to their Christian commitment. The focus group met a number of times before this book was published, and our references to it are intended to raise relevant issues, not necessarily answer them. It was obvious in our focus group discussions that setting godly priorities continues to be a critical area for many Christians in the marketplace.

Snapshots from the Present

Julie is a special education teacher in a suburban school system. She is an excellent teacher and has been recognized by her peers for professional excellence. Julie was divorced several years ago and recently remarried. She has five children, all grown.

Julie talked about her life of a few years ago when her children were young and she was just starting her teaching career. "Back in those days, I would get up early in the morning, try to have a few minutes to myself for a devotional, get the kids up and off to school, and then rush to work myself. I remember praying in the car, asking God just to get me through the day. After work, I would rush home to meet the kids, cook dinner, help them with homework or other projects, do a few chores around the house, and prepare my lesson plans for the next day. This went on for months without a break. Then, on top of all this, we were members of a small church and felt that we needed to do our share in its ministry. I taught Sunday school and was involved in a number of other worthwhile activities."

In looking back, Julie says that she doesn't know how she survived in those days. She gives the Lord the credit but also expresses some regret that she let their church add so many duties to all the other things she was doing. "I'm not sure churches are sensitive to the problems faced by mothers of young children, especially when those mothers find it necessary to work."

Tom is employed by a large national corporation and has a responsible position that requires about 45 hours per week, with occasional travel. He has three children at home, all in elementary or junior high school. Tom says, "My wife and I had been overdoing it with church activities. About a year ago we dropped choir and several other activities. We each now have one activity, and we won't go out more than one night a week. It's difficult to tell people 'no,' but we made up our minds that we had to do it."

Nearly every member of the group cited "being overcommitted in the church" as one of the biggest problems they had in setting priorities in their lives and for their families. Being too busy in their jobs seemed alright, but they expressed resentment about past experiences with over commitment to church work.

Snapshot from the Past:
Boaz Balanced Life Well (Ruth 2—4)

(Note: Please read the entire Scripture portion given in the "Snapshots from the Past" headings as you come to them in each chapter of this book.)

Elimelech and Naomi, along with their two sons, left Bethlehem at the time of a severe famine and journeyed to Moab. While they were there, Elimelech died, and their two sons married Moabite women. Sometime later, Naomi's two sons also died.

Naomi, accompanied by her Moabite daughter-in-law, Ruth, returned to Bethlehem. The two widows arrived in time for the fall harvest. Ruth took advantage of the Israelite custom that permitted the poor to glean grain from nearby fields. Ruth's good fortune began in the fields of Boaz where she was invited to glean (pick up leftover bits of grain left behind by the harvesters) for the entire harvest season.

Boaz was a wealthy farmer and one of Elimelech's relatives. After a time, Naomi instructed Ruth to adhere to the custom of the levirate law (found in Deut. 25) which made provision for a "kinsman-redeemer" to protect a dead man's name and inheritance. Ruth initiated the rite by deciding to lay down on the threshing floor at the feet of Boaz.

The next day, Boaz arranged for the "kinsman-redeemer" issue to be settled at the city gate, where such matters were commonly resolved. After a close relative declined the opportunity to care for Naomi and Ruth, Boaz assumed that responsibility. He then purchased all the property belonging to Elimelech and his sons and married Ruth. Boaz and Ruth became the great grandparents of King David.

Boaz lived out life's priorities well. Although he was a wealthy man, he was kind and generous to the poor of the community. He cared for and protected Ruth's reputation when her actions at the threshing floor might have been misunderstood. At the city gate, he followed God's Word carefully and precisely in selecting someone to care for Naomi and Ruth. And he willingly took up demanding responsibilities without excuses or delays.

Scripture and Personal Application

I Corinthians 10:31 says, "So whether you eat or drink or whatever you do, do it all for the glory of God." This seems to say that whatever we do is okay as long as we are doing it for the glory of God. How does this relate to the problem expressed by several participants in the focus groups: that they resented being overly committed to church work?

Paul, in his Letter to the Philippians, talks about pressing on (Phil. 3:12-14). A pastor, preaching on this text, said that it meant that we should overextend ourselves for Christ. Do you agree or disagree?

In the U. S. it is becoming increasingly difficult for many people to find and hold high-paying jobs. As Christians, should we resist overtime and the other over-and-above commitments which are often required of employees who are on their way up the corporate ladder?

(Read Matt. 6:25-34 and relate it to your work situation.)

Philippians 4:9 says, "Whatever you have learned or received or heard from me, or seen in me—put it into practice." What are some of Paul's personal characteristics that relate to priorities we are called to practice?

Titus 3:14 says, "Our people must learn to devote themselves to doing what is good, in order that they may provide for daily necessities and not live unproductive lives." How can we apply this passage in the affluent society we live in today?

Discussion Questions

(Note: Please consider each of these questions before the class or discussion group for each lesson in this book. Space has been provided for you to note your answers.)

1. What problems have you had in balancing the various parts of your life? This includes time with children, spouse, hobbies, church, work, and recreation. Please share with the group from your personal experience.

2. How have you dealt with these situations? What works and what doesn't work?

3. In light of the experience of Julie and Tom, do you believe it is possible to become overly committed in the church or with religious activities? Explain.

4. Jesus is Lord of your life. How does that fact relate to the various forces pulling at you? Your priorities?

2

DECISION MAKING ON THE JOB

Greg recently resigned from his job as the city manager of a large suburban community to accept a position with an investment banking firm. In reflecting on his 28 years in city administration he said, "I probably made 40 to 50 decisions a day, all of them important in that they affected employees or residents of the city. It would be impossible to pray over each of these decisions. I did try to pray about the overall direction of the city and for wisdom in doing my job, but there is no way I could have stopped for prayer each time it was necessary to decide something."

We have worked with non-Christians whose lives and careers appear, at least on the surface, to represent many intelligent moves or good decisions, some going back to high school and college days (for example, choice of college, major, types of friends). What, then, is different about Christians as they try to live lives characterized by good decisions? Are Christians really better decision makers? Do they take advantage of the wisdom that is available to them through prayer and the Bible?

Snapshots from the Present

John, a physician, noted that it is easy to make decisions in areas that a person has received professional training. He said the big problems he experiences are in areas outside of his sphere of expertise. John said, "Several years ago I built an office building for our practice and to provide rental space for others. But I recently lost the building; my bank took it over. I couldn't find tenants who could pay the rent needed to service my debt on the building. I was in a field—real estate—that I didn't know much about, and I got burned."

Later in the discussion John was asked whether business decisions based on prayer tend to be better decisions than those made without consulting with the Holy Spirit. Despite his problems with the building he owned, he concluded that, yes, he did make better decisions when he asked for the Lord's help and guidance.

Al is the director of development for a Christian college. He recently resigned from a similar, but much higher paying position, with a large university hospital. In reflecting on his decision to change jobs, and seemingly taking a step backward, Al said, "My colleagues in the fund-raising business can't understand what I did. Sometimes I tell them that I am also a consultant, just so they don't think I'm crazy."

Al talked about how the process of making this major decision affected his career and his family. "Of course, our decision to go into this form of full-time Christian ministry wasn't taken lightly. My wife and I talked about it for months and years. In effect, we said to God, "We are available, use us." We opened ourselves up to the leading of the Holy Spirit, but we had nothing specific in mind. When an offer came from the Christian college, we were prepared to make the move. Even though the new job has significantly lowered our income, we are enjoying ourselves and are confident that we did the right thing."

A recently retired executive with a large banking system told us, "Adversity is a great learning tool for helping us make better decisions in our business. It makes us humble. The worst thing we can do, especially if we are in a position of responsibility, is to become too cocky, to think we know it all. This is a sure formula for disaster." He also pointed out that bankers need to be right in their loan decisions, or the organization will not survive. "If we don't bat 98 percent in our decisions on loans, we won't make it." He went on to say that the character of the people asking for money is often a key factor considered in making a loan, especially to a small business.

Major Issues

In the course of listening and reacting to these examples, the group discussed several issues relating to decision making. What role does a spouse play in making decisions that affect the family? Several noted, for example, that it is not wise for a man to miss out on the intuitive approach that many women bring to the decision-making process.

Larry Burkett, a well-known author and speaker on the subject of Christians in business, emphasizes the importance of husbands seeking input from wives before making major business-oriented decisions. He places a high value on the intuitive approach women may use in making decisions, and he holds the opinion, based on his experience with hundreds of businessmen, that men miss the boat by not taking advantage of this resource.

Along the same line, the group talked about the value of seeking outside counsel in making important decisions. Greg, the former city administrator, said that he talked to his brother and two other men, whose opinions he had learned to trust, before making the decision to change jobs. He said, "I wouldn't undertake a change of this magnitude without consulting with my wife, whose opinion I value tremendously—and other trusted advisors."

The unique advantages a Christian has in making important decisions were discussed in detail, and the consensus was that these advantages exist and are important. The inner peace that comes from being in God's will has been experienced by several of the participants. The ability to view a decision, or the results of a decision, in a broader context was extremely valuable.

How do you monitor the quality of your decisions after they have been made? There were differences of opinion on this question. Several members of the group said that they do not look back and try to second guess themselves. These individuals recognize that not all of their decisions, even when based on prayer, are going to be the best that can be made. Others raised the question: "What criteria would be applied to help you see if past decisions were the best possible under the circumstances?" One person said, "What may appear to be a bad decision based on worldly standards may, in fact, turn out to be pleasing in God's sight. So, why go crazy by looking back and second guessing yourself, or being too introspective?"

**Snapshot from the Past:
Solomon's Decisions (I Ki. 3)**

Solomon was the tenth son of King David and the second son of Bathsheba. He was not the obvious heir apparent to his father's throne. However, after some struggles and battles, Solomon successfully succeeded his father as king.

A significant spiritual experience occurred in Solomon's life while he was worshiping at Gibeon, a few miles northwest of Jerusalem. God appeared to Solomon in a dream and asked him what he wanted from the Lord. Instead of asking for selfish things, the young king requested practical wisdom to govern his people properly and justly.

The Lord was pleased by Solomon's request for wisdom, and He graciously granted Solomon his wish. The Lord added riches and honor to Solomon's life and promised him a long life if he walked with and obeyed the Lord as David had done.

Not long after this experience, two mothers stood before King Solomon, each claiming that the same baby was her own. There were no witnesses. A modern judge might have dismissed the case for lack of evidence. Solomon, however, quickly devised a plan that restored the baby to its real mother. When news of his wise decision passed quickly throughout the land, the people realized that Solomon "had wisdom from God to administer justice" (I Kings 3:28).

Solomon petitioned the Lord for wisdom. The Lord answered Solomon's request, and he became a fine administrator and an excellent decision-maker.

Scripture and Personal Application

Matthew 25:14-30 describes an investment decision: the parable of a man going on a journey and trusting his servants to make good use of his financial resources while he was away. Two of the servants made wise decisions, which undoubtedly involved risk, and the third decided to sit on what he had been given. There are many aspects to this parable, but focus on the decision-making processes of the three servants. How did they decide what to do? How did the first two servants know what their master expected? And, why did the third servant so badly misjudge what he should have done with the talents? (In this case the results of the decision making by the servants are known, both in terms of the success or failure of their investment decisions and whether or not they were pleasing to the master.)

Decision making for the Christian has a lot to do with wisdom, something the Bible mentions often. Read Proverbs 4:1-17. What are the applications (regarding decision making in the workplace) from this chapter?

Romans 12:2 says, "Do not conform any longer to the pattern of this world, but be transformed by the renewing of your mind. Then you will be able to test and approve what God's will is—his good, pleasing and perfect will."

Chapters 1 and 2 of I Corinthians tell us much about the superiority of God's wisdom compared with human wisdom. Read these two chapters and identify ways the truths presented can be used to make better decisions, both at work and in personal matters.

Is James 1:5-8 applicable here? How should these verses be put into practice?

Colossians 3:17 says, "And whatever you do, whether in word or deed, do it all in the name of the Lord Jesus, giving thanks to God the Father through him." How does this passage relate to decision making on the job?

Read Acts 16:6-10. These verses mention twice that the Holy Spirit gave Paul and his companions direction in what to do and where to go on their missionary journey. How does the Holy Spirit influence your decisions at work?

In Luke 6:12-16, we are told that Jesus spent a night praying before He chose His 12 disciples. What part does prayer play in your decision-making process?

"Plans fail for lack of counsel, but with many advisers they succeed" (Prov. 15:22). How does the use of advisers help in making decisions? Share your experience.

Colossians 1:9, 10 expresses the foundation for godly decision making. How could you apply this text to your decisions at work?

Read Acts 15. A disagreement arose in the early Christian church between Jewish and Gentile believers. The apostles and elders met to consider solutions to this sharp division. After a lengthy discussion, Peter spoke (vs. 7). Also, Barnabas and Paul addressed the assembly (vs. 12). After listening to all of this, James proposed a solution (vs. 13 ff). When the church received this decision, they were glad and encouraged (vs. 31 ff). What important steps were taken in the decision-making process in this case? How are these steps applicable to your work situation?

Discussion Questions

1. What are the types of decisions you typically make at work? Do you make a large number of relatively unimportant decisions, or a few significant ones? Explain.

2. How does your personal decision-making process differ from that of those you work with? Does being a Christian make any difference? If so, how? Please be specific.

3. Lots of good decision makers use all the available facts as well as intuition. Bob Waterman, in his book *The Renewal Factor*, talks about top executives using their "gut" in making decisions. As a Christian, what does it mean to you to rely on the guidance of the Holy Spirit to know how to make a particular decision? Discuss some specific ways of making ourselves available to the Spirit's guidance.

4. In looking back on your life decisions, how do you know when you have made a good decision? What criteria should we apply in judging our past decisions?

3

ACHIEVING EXCELLENCE ON THE JOB

Excellence has been a very popular word in the 1980's. The most widely read business book ever printed, *In Search of Excellence,* focused the business community's attention on the need to improve quality and offered tips from America's best-run companies on how to do it.

Another business phrase often heard in the past five years is "competitive advantage." Many businesses, and non-profit organizations as well, have been seeking ways to gain competitive advantage. Michael Porter, a well-known Harvard Business School professor and consultant, popularized this phrase, and has written two books on how organizations can differentiate themselves in order to compete more successfully.

A major factor in the current concern over excellence, or quality, has come about because of competition from the Japanese. In the view of many, Japanese automobiles and electronic equipment have far exceeded the quality and performance of competitive U. S. products. Numerous articles and books have been written and many theories advanced on how we can compete with overseas suppliers of goods and services.

But where does our Christian faith fit into this emphasis on excellence, productivity, and competition? We are taught in the Scriptures that the local body of Christ thrives when all members (or parts of the body) work together using the gifts God has provided. How can businessmen and women, and others who work, shift gears from functioning in an increasingly competitive marketplace to one that stresses cooperation and the use of spiritual gifts?

Snapshots from the Present

On the question of productivity, many workers and managers face the issue, "How much is enough?" Tom, who works for a large aerospace company says, "I could stay at work every day from six in the morning until seven at night and not get everything done. I've had to learn to let the phone ring as I'm walking out the door to go home." Has his new attitude toward work had a negative impact on his chances for salary increases and opportunities for advancement? "Probably, but there are things that are more important to me than more money and prestige. As long as I can walk out the door and feel good about myself, that I've put in a good effort during the time I'm supposed to be in my office, I'm satisfied."

Don, an entrepreneur, said that he feels we should use the talents God has given us to their maximum. "But," he says, "we can only control our *efforts,* not the *results*. Starting a new business from scratch is a lot like witnessing to people about Christ. We are obligated to witness, but the Holy Spirit is responsible for the results. This takes the pressure off of us. Starting a business is the same. If we are interested in a sure thing, we won't try it. By its very nature, there is substantial risk of failure. But I feel, and my family agrees, that we should try to take advantage of the opportunity God seems to have placed before us. Anyway, it's His business, so we aren't uptight."

Several focus group participants commented on the issue of how much we should concern ourselves with results rather than just focusing on our efforts. Those people in marketing or sales occupations were especially sensitive to this question. One person said, "My partners agreed to my proposal that we start a new health care product line. They have spent a lot of the company's earnings to fund this new venture. I've taken several expensive marketing trips visiting hospitals all over the country, and so far we haven't generated the business we expected. I'm concerned, but reconciled to the fact that I've done the best I can; I can't do any more."

Is this a cop-out, or a valid way to assess our efforts in spite of the lack of projected returns to our employers? While most Christians may be sympathetic to "I've done the best I can," others may not be as satisfied with it, particularly if it affects their own income or net worth.

Another issue discussed was whether we ought to call attention to our accomplishments or to the quality and productivity of our work. Should a Christian worker toot his or her own horn in order to get a salary increase, bonus, or promotion? Isn't it enough just to do a good job and let the chips fall where they may? What about those people in a marketing or related business where it is important to sell the capabilities of the product in order to win a contract or get an order? Shouldn't Christians in business be humble about their accomplishments?

Greg offered these thoughts: "I never liked it when employees called attention to themselves; it rubbed me the wrong way. I guess I believe that over a period of time good or excellent performance will stand out without the individual having to call attention to himself." Greg did acknowledge that when he applied for his present job he prepared a resume highlighting his accomplishments. "I feel that preparing a resume is different. It is supposed to be an honest recap of a person's accomplishments and experience. Obviously, we shouldn't exaggerate what we have done. But, there are times when it is necessary to lay it out in black and white."

Keith Miller, in his book *A Taste of New Wine* devoted a

chapter to the idea of bringing God into the business office. He described how he prayed for creativity and the ability to accomplish specific tasks quickly and without errors. One of the focus group participants shared his experience. "I have prayed for Christ to help me get a job done under extreme time pressures and to have the creativity and openness of mind to do the job very well. Based on my experience, He answers that kind of prayer."

Another person shared how he learned to shorten his perspective on work time as he gained experience. "I've found that I have to approach a project one day at a time. If I think in terms of a 60- or 90-day time period to get a job done, I tend to waste the first 30 or 45 days and rely on my ability to make it up later. But this is a dangerous approach and one that isn't fair to my employer or my family; it is too crisis-oriented. Each day is important, and what we accomplish over a long period is nothing more than the accumulation of a number of single days of effort."

What It Means to Be a Winner

In his book, *For Men Only,* J. Allan Petersen quoted an unknown author in describing the characteristics of a winner. A winner:

- Respects those who are superior to him and tries to learn something from them.
- Says, "Let's find a way"; a loser says, "There is no way."
- Goes through a problem; a loser goes around the problem.
- Says, "There should be a better way to do it"; a loser says, "That's the way it's always been done."
- Works harder than a loser, and has more time; a loser is always too busy to do what is necessary.
- Makes commitments; a loser makes promises.

PROV 16: 1-4

Scripture and Personal Application

Colossians 3:23-25 tells us to work with all our heart, as if working for the Lord rather than working merely for people. The Bible extols quality of work but not for the same reasons that most Americans desire quality in their work. How can this concept be applied in the workplace?

I Corinthians 3:12-15 provides a Christian perspective on work. Does this passage apply to our "church" work only, or to all of the work that we perform? How do we know that the type of work we are doing has long-term, or eternal, value? If we are dissatisfied with the type of work we do, or the permanence of its value, what can we do about it? How do we balance the responsibility to provide for our families with the desire to do meaningful work?

Proverbs 14:23 says that " All hard work brings a profit, but mere talk leads only to poverty." Many of us have jobs in which we are required to attend numerous meetings and spend a high proportion of our time talking and listening. How do you reconcile these kinds of jobs with the wisdom contained in this verse?

Colossians 3:23, 24 says, "Whatever you do, work at it with all your heart, as working for the Lord, not men, since you know that you will receive an inheritance from the Lord as a reward. It is the Lord Christ you are serving." In the routine of daily work, how do you remember this? What might help remind you of the principle?

"Whatever your hand finds to do, do it with all your might" (Eccl. 9:10). How does this verse relate to what we are discussing in this chapter?

Discussion Questions

1. How do you try to demonstrate excellence on the job? What are some areas where you might improve?

2. If you were hiring a new employee, what personal qualities of excellence would you look for? As an employee, what qualities and attitudes of excellence do you expect from your boss?

3. In an increasingly competitive world economy, your employer considers it important that you help your organization gain a competitive advantage. But when you gain, do others lose? Economic theory suggests that this type of competition is for the "greater good" because it weeds out the less efficient producers. What is your perspective on this sort of competitive environment and the role you must play if you are to keep your job?

4. Most Americans accept the notion that it is wise to invest in education and training in order to enhance skills and earning power. This will make us more valuable in the job market. You have probably observed, first hand, the differences that education and training can make in terms of income and quality of life. If you are a Christian preparing yourself for a career, what should be your motivation for improving and broadening your appeal to potential employers?

4

THE IMPORTANCE OF PLANNING

Should a Christian worker or business manager become involved in long-range planning and goal setting? This question has often intrigued us, especially in light of James 4:13-17:

Now listen, you who say, "Today or tomorrow we go to this or that city, spend a year there, carry on business and make money. Why, you do not even know what will happen tomorrow. What is your life? You are a mist that appears for a little while and then vanishes. Instead, you ought to say, "If it is the Lord's will, we will live and do this or that." As it is, you boast and brag. All such boasting is evil. Anyone, then, who knows the good he ought to do and doesn't do it, sins.

Given these words, how does the American business preoccupation with strategic planning stack up? Another common phrase, "the bottom line," is often used to judge whether a plan should be implemented. Is "management by objectives" consistent with the teachings of James?

If we assume that it is alright for a Christian to be involved in some level of planning, what perspective should be brought to bear on the planning process? Bob Waterman, in his book *The Renewal Factor* says it is okay for organizations to plan, just as long as they don't take their plans too seriously. He goes on to point out that the main value in strategic planning is that it gets people to communicate and to share information, values, and objectives. In other words, the "process" is ultimately more important than the product. Often the only tangible by-product of a planning process is a lengthy document that collects dust. But the intangibles of increased communication and overall sense of direction can be invaluable.

Snapshots from the Present

"I don't mind planning as such, but the way it is done in my company is an exercise in futility. People seem to be more interested in filling out forms than in doing anything productive." The person making this observation works for a large corporation.

"It drives me crazy to work in a place where they don't plan," said a woman who had worked as an office manager for a variety of firms. "I worked in a real estate sales office where they just sat around and waited for the phone to ring; this is no way to run a business. We needed a plan to generate sales, and someone who would move ahead with it.

"One purpose of planning is to give us greater control over our destinies. I can see that as being in conflict with the idea that we as Christians should be sensitive, moment by moment, to the leading of the Holy Spirit. But should a Christian just turn everything over to God and say, 'I'll just flow with the Spirit'?

"I've seen companies that used planning as a way to control their employees. And that *is* one way to get things done. I used to work for a company that operated in this way, and I didn't like it." These comments were made by an entrepreneur. He went on to say, "As Christians, we are to seek God's leading; we are to live our lives in ways that are consistent with His plan. But that doesn't mean we sit around and do nothing. We need to figure out what He wants us to do, and then do it."

The group spent several minutes talking about personal business and financial planning, particularly as it is carried out by Christians. One person observed, "There seem to be two extremes among the Christians I know. Some people are very well organized and appear to have their finances and other aspects of their lives under control. At the other extreme are the people who want to be open to the leading of the Holy Spirit and who are afraid that laying concrete plans will inhibit the Spirit's work."

Another person observed that the lack of planning in an individual's life seems to run counter to the concept of God being the Lord of our lives, including our finances, time, energies, and families. To be a good manager, investments need to be made prudently, and resources allocated in ways that will please the Lord. "All of this implies a certain amount of planning and long-range goal setting," he said.

Chuck said, "I am not, by nature, a planner. I approach life on a very flexible and short-term basis. But my wife and I have been in a Bible study where we have been going through the Book of Nehemiah. When we started, I couldn't see spending more than a couple of sessions on this book. But as we got into it, I began to get a vision of the tremendous amount of planning that Nehemiah did, and I gained a new respect for the ability to look ahead and figure out what to do over a long period on a large, complex project."

Another person told the story of a friend of his who had been in the construction business in Oregon. This individual lost his job but made no effort to find a new one. "The Lord will take care of me," he said. He eventually lost his home and wife but continued to wait patiently—and pray—for a new job. "I felt sorry for him and talked to him several times. It didn't do any good; he knew what he wanted to do and there was nothing I could say that would change his mind."

How does planning in a Christian organization differ from planning in the corporate world? One of the authors, who is director of development for a seminary, said that his organization plans for the future in ways comparable to those used by businesses. "We have to be sensitive to God's leading, but we do this by talking to people, by carefully assessing our financial and human resources, and by praying. Right now we are considering a multimillion-dollar building project, and I'm responsible for figuring out how we are going to pay for it. This involves lots of travel and contact with potential donors; we have to find out whether or not they feel led to support this project before we can make a decision to proceed. Since the new building will be used for many years, we have to predict our future enrollment and faculty size, and we have to anticipate other needs likely to develop over the years."

"My definition of a successful person is someone who is working toward a goal," said one person. "The specific nature of that goal is less important than the fact that the individual has an objective. As Christians, our overall goals should be to lead lives that are pleasing to God. Non-Christians lack this goal. Yet, I still prefer dealing with a person who has some goals in life, even strictly secular goals. And I think we have a better chance of reaching these kinds of people for Christ because at least they are thinking about the future."

Frank said, "People in the secular world have a general knowledge of Christian or Scriptural principles and they use them. We have this same base of knowledge, but we also have the power of prayer. That is what makes the difference in our planning and decision making."

Greg pointed out another advantage for Christians—patience. "Christians should have more patience and more understanding when plans go awry. We shouldn't get as uptight or as bent out of shape when things don't work out."

One major advantage Christians have in planning is a broader, more realistic perspective about the future and where their lives or their businesses fit into the total scheme of things. Sometimes we are accused of being unrealistic, but if we accept the Bible as the fundamental truth governing our lives—and our businesses—we should enjoy a more realistic view of the future and how best to achieve our goals in this future environment.

Snapshot from the Past:
Nehemiah Planned and Built the Wall (Neh. 2:11-20)

Prayer and planning go together. Nehemiah was a first-class planner who knew the importance of planning and prayer. He showed both of these disciplines in his ability to plan and in his courage as he took action.

Nehemiah spent four months in fervent prayer before he made his request to King Artaxerxes—asking to go to Jerusalem to restore the dignity of his ancestral home. Often Nehemiah's first impulse was to pray before taking action (Neh. 1:4; 2:4; 4:4, 9; 6:9, 14).

Arriving in Jerusalem, he privately surveyed the work that needed to be done. He encouraged the religious and political leaders with his report and plan. Then, he skillfully organized the community to carry out the effort of rebuilding the broken wall.

In spite of repeated external and internal opposition, Nehemiah executed his plan. Some of his enemies attempted to slow down production by insulting and mocking him. Others tried armed attacks and gossip. Although his enemies were successful in hindering and stopping the work for a time, Nehemiah continually demonstrated his powerful leadership qualities and organizational abilities.

Because of Nehemiah's prayers, efficient planning, and successful execution of his plans, the wall was completed in 52 days.

If you are convinced that your plan is good and you are "prayed up," do you give in when the going gets tough? Nehemiah hung in there, in spite of powerful opposition, until he completed his project. How might you go about developing some of Nehemiah's characteristics in your own life?

Scripture and Personal Application

Proverbs 16:3 says, "Commit to the Lord whatever you do, and your plans will succeed." On the positive side, the passage implies that we should plan, that we shouldn't go through life, or our work, without a plan of action pretty well thought through. But this sounds too easy. Have you ever tried this, only to have your plans appear to fail? How do you explain this?

Proverbs 15:22 says, "Plans fail for lack of counsel, but with many advisers they succeed." Our experience in business is that it is more difficult to plan with the involvement of many people, but the planning process has a better chance of being implemented if many persons have been consulted. The Japanese are noted for involving large numbers of employees in planning; it appears to be inefficient, but the results tend to justify the wisdom of this approach. In your personal planning, or at work, how do you go about seeking the opinions and involvement of others?

Some frequently quoted verses, Romans 8:28, 37, say that we are more than conquerors because "we know that in all things God works for the good of those who love him, who have been called according to his purpose." While this is a comforting verse when we have made mistakes or are hurting, is this a reason for not trying to make good decisions or for not taking our personal or business planning seriously? Explain.

____

____

____

____

____

Another proverb notes that if you "trust in the Lord with all your heart and lean not on your own understanding; in all your ways acknowledge him, . . . he will make your paths straight" (Prov. 3:5, 6). Proverbs 16:9 says, "In his heart a man plans his course, but the Lord determines his steps."

Luke 14:28-30 says, "Suppose one of you wants to build a tower. Will he not first sit down and estimate the cost to see if he has enough money to complete it? For if he lays the foundation and is not able to finish it, everyone who sees it will ridicule him saying, 'This fellow began to build and was not able to finish.'" Isn't it true today that when we see a partially completed building or construction project deteriorating over the years that we tend to frown upon the individuals or corporations behind it? This passage sounds like we need to incorporate economic and financial considerations into the planning process. What do you think? Why?

____

____

____

____

How does Proverbs 19:21 relate to the foregoing verse?

Read Jeremiah 29:11-13. What things can you do to help yourself live out God's plan for your work?

I Corinthians 14:40 was given in the context of Paul's discussion of proper worship. Is the concept of performing all kinds of work in "a fitting and orderly way" also consistent with New Testament principles? Explain.

Proverbs 21:30 says, "There is no wisdom, no insight, no plan that can succeed against the Lord." How do you know when your work or business plans are not "against the Lord?" Share your personal experience in this area.

Discussion Questions

1. What kind of planning do you do in your business or profession? How formal or informal is it? What is your planning horizon or time frame?

2. How does your faith in Christ and your reliance on the leading of the Holy Spirit affect the way you plan in your business? How about your personal or family financial planning?

3. How do you react when your plans don't materialize?

4. In your life, what is the balance between planning and action? Is the balance what you think it should be?

5. How do you relate long-range planning and goal-setting to the Biblical concept of stewardship? For you, are the two interrelated?

5

SUPERVISOR-EMPLOYEE RELATIONSHIPS

This chapter deals with the unique problems experienced by Christians when they supervise others or are employees. In the focus group discussion that formed the basis for part of this chapter, much of our conversation dealt with the supervisor's perspective. The points that were raised, however, are equally relevant to those who are being supervised. What difference does being a Christian make in how you manage your employees? What difference does it make in how you relate to your boss?

Snapshots from the Present

"I don't think you can generalize about an employee's performance on the basis of whether or not he or she is a Christian." This was the opinion of a former public official. "I've often had higher expectations for my Christian employees, but I've learned not to get my hopes up. I've been disappointed too many times."

This person went on to tell about one of his assistants, a Christian, who he felt took advantage of the relationship. "This fellow would do irritating and unproductive things, like consistently coming late to staff meetings. I don't know why he did it; I guess he thought that he could take advantage of me and that I wouldn't do anything about it.

"One time there was a secretary, a Christian, who

worked for a person under me. I had excellent rapport with this woman and she shared a lot about what was going on in the organization. Unfortunately, other secretaries got wind of this and it created an awkward situation. I had to stop talking to this person."

Tom, who works for a large company, said he has had a Christian working for him and that he had a very special relationship with this person. "One time this fellow came in and talked to me about a job offer in another city. We prayed about it, and I recommended that he take it." Tom went on to say that the relationship had never created jealousy among other employees. "I really valued our relationship," he said.

Don, who has his own company, a high-tech start-up venture, noted that in judging Christian employees we need to recognize the various levels of Christian maturity in people. "Some brand new Christians are not going to act much differently than they did before they were saved. We make a mistake in expecting these people to perform at a maturity level that is way above them. On the other hand, we have every right to have higher expectations of more mature brothers and sisters in Christ."

Issues for the Christian Employer and Employee

Are professing Christians, who are supervisors, under pressure to perform at higher levels than other managers? Are Christian managers supposed to have better control of their tempers? Should they be more compassionate? Be less demanding? Have greater integrity?

Several in the group admitted that they had, on several occasions, lost their tempers with one of their employees. However, there was a difference of opinion on whether this was good or bad. One person said, "I tried, for many years, to control my temper. Then my wife once asked me why I held back. Reflecting on her comment, I agreed that I shouldn't suppress my feelings. Since that time I have gotten very upset at what I considered to be poor or unacceptable performance, and I let the employee know it in no uncertain terms. I feel better about myself when I let these employees know how I feel. I feel I owe it to them to let them know."

Chuck told about several instances where he had blown up at an employee. "After it happened and I had a chance to think about it, I felt bad. In fact, in nearly every case I called up the person at home at night and apologized. The Bible says that we shouldn't let the sun set on our anger and that we should get things resolved as soon as possible. I feel this approach works for me."

The delicate issue of how to relate to employees in terms of showing our humanness or frailties was also discussed. One person said, "I've noticed that when you give people the impression that you have your life under control, that you have your act together, very few people come to you to share their problems. On the other hand, those persons whose lives are filled with difficulties seem to attract a following of others who want to share their personal problems." As supervisors, what sort of face do we present? How approachable do we want to be? The conventional wisdom, at least in some quarters, is that a manager shouldn't become too involved with employees and their problems. Is this a valid option for Christians who supervise others?

Tom shared with the group that he had been downgraded at work because of his tendency to let his feelings show. "I tend to let it all hang out; that's the way I am. My boss says that my behavior is sometimes unprofessional, and he has reproved me for it. But I don't plan to change. I'm going to be myself; I'm not going to put on an act. Life is too short for that."

Don felt there is a delicate balance in how much of ourselves we reveal to our employees. There are real dangers, he said, in going too far in terms of letting employees see into every nook and cranny of our personalities and lives. On the other hand, we don't want to appear to be "holier than thou," or that we are immune from problems.

Another person talked about the need for supervisors to be honest with their employees, especially in sharing about employee performance. "Employees are usually hungry for feedback on how well they are doing their jobs. We have an obligation to provide this in an honest and straightforward way."

What are the most important things a Christian supervisor brings to the job that might be absent in a non-Christian manager? One person said that prayer for employees is the most important contribution that a Christian can make in improving supervisor-employee relationships. "When I pray for an employee, the Lord often gives me a different perspective about that person, and I tend to have a much greater ability to see the situation from that employee's point of view." Tom agreed, saying, "When I'm praying for my employees, I am much more sensitive about my effect on these people as their manager. I listen better. I care more about them."

Snapshot from the Past: Daniel the Prophet (Dan. 6)

The following is quoted from *Marketplace Networks*, January, 1988, a publication of InterVarsity Christian Fellowship.

Daniel's bosses were every bit as tough to work for as yours. They were constantly afraid of losing their own jobs, and tended to evaluate everything Daniel did in terms of how good it made them look. They were gullible—believing everything their boss said as if it were written in stone. And worst of all, Daniel's supervisors were absolutely vicious towards employees who didn't measure up—even to the point of throwing them in jail.

Clearly, Daniel would have felt right at home in the modern, secular workplace—the problems are all too familiar. You might even identify with his particular career path. Because even though Daniel is often described as a prophet, his first job was actually as a trainee, or intern, in government business. Before long he developed strong skills as an analyst and coun-

selor. Eventually he grew into a management role, first under Nebuchadnezzar, then under Belshazzar, and finally under King Darius.

In fact, Daniel became so well-respected for his abilities that from time to time he was called on to be a negotiator between competitive or even warring factions.

So in spite of his hostile, sometimes terrifying work environment, Daniel managed to build a distinguished career. He had a profound impact on the system, and even won the full admiration and respect of his employers.

Scripture and Personal Application

Ephesians 6:5-9 describes the relationship between master and slave. How do you see the points included in these verses on respect, sincerity of heart, obedience, and serving wholeheartedly relating to the employee-supervisor relationship today? Verse 7 suggests that we are working for the Lord, not someone else. If you agree with this, how does it affect your attitude toward work?

____

____

____

The passages conclude by saying that masters should have the same attitudes toward their slaves and should show no favoritism.

Read Exodus 18:13-27. This passage describes how Moses organized the Israelites in order to have a functioning nation and not wear himself out. This is a good example of the delegation of responsibility and authority that is just as applicable today as it was in the time of Moses. What are some major differences between a good organization and a bad one?

____

____

____

In Acts 6:1-7 we have an example of organization in the early church. There was a division of responsibility and delegation of authority to various individuals. There were supervisors and individuals being supervised. Do you think there were ever problems? Inept supervisors? Ineffective employees? How do you think the early church leaders would have tried to resolve these problems?

____

____

____

Philippians 2:14, 15 states, "Do everything without complaining or arguing, so that you may become blameless and pure, children of God without fault in a crooked and depraved generation, in which you shine like stars in the universe." How would you apply this text to supervisor-employee relationships?

____

____

The organization of the New Testament church is a model that is applicable to churches and many other organizations today. Read I Corinthians 12:12-31. This passage clearly illustrates that we all have different capabilities, or gifts, and that there has to be an organized approach to reaching people and performing the various ministries of the church. Do the same principles apply to your firm or business organization? If so, how?

____

____

____

____

Are there other good examples of proper organization, and the relationship between supervisors and employees in the Bible? Give one or two other examples.

Discussion Questions

1. What has been your personal experience in either supervising others or being supervised? Which situation do you prefer? Why?

2. Do your employees and/or employers know you are a Christian? If so, how do you believe this affects their perceptions of you? Give examples.

3. Do you have special bonds with one or more Christians you work with, either above you, below you, or at the same level as you in the organization? Does your position in the organization affect the depth of sharing between the two of you?

4. What are your expectations of a Christian employee?

What are your expectations of a Christian boss?

5. Have you ever witnessed or been involved in a situation where favoritism between a supervisor and an employee was shown? How did you *feel* about it? What did you *do* about it?

6. Is there a difference between Christian and non-Christian employees in terms of their response to various methods of motivation? Explain.

7. How should one's Christianity affect the way he or she *disciplines* an employee? How should it affect the way he or she *motivates* an employee?

6

WHEN HUSBAND AND WIFE BOTH WORK

Over 60 percent of the mothers in the U.S. with children under 14 years of age are in the labor force. Seven out of ten of these mothers work because they must help support their families. For many families the middle income dream of a house, a car and three square meals for the kids carries this dual income requirement. These are some of the conclusions from a *Time* magazine article of June 22, 1987. "What was once a problem only of poor families has now become a part of daily life and a basic concern of typical American families," says the article in quoting a Columbia University professor of social policy and planning.

A *Denver Post* article in October 1987 said that competitive pressures on businesses in the U. S. are damaging families. "Competition is pressuring American businesses into a survival mentality which is damaging families and communities. . . . Competitive pressures translate to work overload, lack of control over one's job, and unsupportive supervisors. . . . This is compounded by the need for many women to enter careers and balance job and family . . . while child-care facilities are lacking."

Discussing stress in families where both husband and wife work, *The Wall Street Journal* says that although both mothers and fathers experience stress, ". . . working mothers usually lead the stress sweepstakes. The Boston University survey, like others before it, found that the total time spent on combined job and family demands is 'considerably greater' for women than for men."

We chose to include a chapter on this subject because we felt it is a matter of importance to large numbers of Christian families where both the husband and wife find it necessary, or desirable, to be in the workplace. For Christians, as well as others, this sort of situation creates special stresses that were less common 20 or 30 years ago.

Snapshots from the Present

Lisa, the mother of three school-age children, is an intensive care nurse at a community hospital. She says that she is physically tired much of the time, but because of economic pressure, she must continue to work. "I would much rather stay home and take care of my family, but I can't do it and probably won't be able to for several more years. It all depends on how quickly my husband can get on his feet career wise."

Lisa went on to say that a big part of her ability to survive over the past 14 years of full-time, demanding work as a nurse has been the time she has spent each day in prayer. "Without this quiet time I know I would have broken, either physically or emotionally. The Lord has really blessed me during this time, and He has given me the strength I need to continue."

Mary, a school teacher, is the mother of three boys and a girl, and has worked most of the time they were growing up. Mary said, "I have worked partly out of economic necessity but mainly because of the professional challenge; I love teaching, and that is what I'm trained for. Being a teacher made it a little easier in that I typically get home by 4:00 p.m.; this gives me a little more time with my family than I would have in many other kinds of work situations." Mary went on to say that her biggest frustration was the difficulty of finding quality people to take care of the kids when they were small. "When we were first married and lived in Southern California, I could call on my mother in an emergency. But when we moved to Colorado, I didn't have someone to step in when the kids were sick or other emergencies came along."

Joanne worked off and on when her two children were young. She agreed with Mary about the problems of finding dependable baby sitters. She added, "My biggest frustration was the feeling of never being caught up. I could never get my housework done. You work an eight-hour day and then you've got another five hours on top of that just to stay even, not to let the mess get any worse. It takes its toll. There was never enough time to do the things we wanted to do." She added, "Now that our kids are grown, I'm enjoying getting back to work. I need the contact with adults. And yes, I am caught up with my housework!"

Ted, who owns a small consulting firm with his wife and another partner, said that he and his wife have been working together for the past 18 months and they really enjoy it. "This is the first time we have had the opportunity to do something like this, and it seems to be working out for both of us. She understands my problems—or I should say our problems—in ways that are new and different. I praise the Lord that we have this opportunity to work together."

Major Issues

What kind of support do women who work receive from their churches? Don said, "We were told, in pretty strong terms, by a deacon of our church that my wife should *not* be working. He said she should be home with our children." Joanne added, "I felt this kind of pressure from several church members some years ago, but I think attitudes have changed in recent years and this sort of thing has become more common." Lisa, on the other hand, said that their family situation was so desperate some years ago that church members urged her to use her skills as a nurse to help support the family financially. Mary followed up by saying that the approval or disapproval of women working seems to be related to the profession of the woman. "If you are a teacher or a nurse, it seems to be okay."

Several members of the group discussed how a husband and wife can work together in sharing the household chores. They agreed that wives who want their husbands to help around the house have to be flexible about how the jobs get done. One person said, "One of our first big fights was over how my husband folded the laundry. But now I realize that's not very important; I've learned that if he is going to help—and he is willing to do almost anything—I can't expect him to do things the same way I do."

One of the women shared, "I've always been a perfectionist on housework. But, when I had to go to work, things began to slide. My husband tried to help, but he just couldn't seem to do things the way I wanted them done. I finally learned to relax and to flow with the situation. Yes, our house is messy, at least by my personal standards, but I recognize that being able to work together is more important." Chuck agreed. He said, "Why do people feel that their houses have to be in such great shape that if the President walked in, he would be impressed?"

Does the Christian family have special resources available to help them deal with the stresses created when both husband and wife work, especially when there are small children at home? Several members of the group cited personal experiences in support of an affirmative answer. Don said, "I believe that God actually gives a person additional reserves of strength and energy simply because he asks. I've cried so hard I couldn't see, and gone for long walks, praying the whole time, just to ask the Lord to give me the ability to go on. And, over and over again, He gives me the strength I need." Don went on, "As men, we often don't like to admit our weaknesses; we have a harder time asking for help than do women. But God will honor our humility and give us supernatural power when we ask."

There are differing attitudes on how the funds generated by both husband and wife should be managed. Some couples pool everything, while others keep all or part of the funds separate, designated for different uses. One person said, "I've seen some two-income couples treat their earnings like roommates do; each pays certain bills, and the monies are not intermingled." Questions were raised about how this related to Biblical principles of stewardship.

Frequent business travel often creates problems for younger couples with children, especially when the trips are for extended periods. These problems can be even more severe for a two-income family. One individual said, "There is no simple answer to this problem. One thing that helps is keeping your mate fully informed about where you are and what you are doing. Several years ago a friend who traveled a lot told me that he called home every night. I started doing it and it really helped. My wife knows that I will be calling in and that we can discuss problems or special situations. We feel more in touch."

Snapshot from the Past:
Aquila and Priscilla Worked (Acts 18)

Because the emperor Claudius didn't like Jews, he expelled them from Rome. Aquila and Priscilla were among those who were forced to leave. They migrated toward Asia Minor, Aquila's known homeland. Undoubtedly, they left behind several of their friends and some of their possessions. They settled in Corinth and began working there.

Both Aquila and Priscilla were tentmakers by trade. Paul, a tentmaker as well, met them in Corinth. They worked together, and Aquila and Priscilla supplied gracious hospitality for Paul.

Later, Priscilla and Aquila accompanied Paul to Ephesus. They probably moved their business again, and later Paul continued on his way. At Ephesus, Priscilla and Aquila met Apollos and invited him to their home, where they had a special, spiritual ministry to him.

Priscilla and Aquila had several opportunities to use their home as a place of ministry. The Ephesian church met there (I Cor. 16:19), and later the Roman church enjoyed their hospitality as well (Rom. 16:4).

It seems that Priscilla and Aquila functioned harmoniously together in their tentmaking business and as partners in ministry offering hospitality in their home. It appears that they were able to blend their work and ministry into an effective life-style.

Aquila and Priscilla worked together as a husband-and-wife team. Explain how their lives would have been different if Priscilla had worked outside their home for someone else. What stresses would they have encountered?

____

____

____

____

Scripture and Personal Application

Read Proverbs 31:10-31 on the role of wife and mother. Describe how a woman can carry on a full-time job and still meet the expectations of this passage. You may use your own experience as an example.

"Do not wear yourself out to get rich; have the wisdom to show restraint. Cast but a glance at riches, and they are gone, for they will surely sprout wings and fly off to the sky like an eagle" (Prov. 23:4, 5). How does this passage relate to the question of both husband and wife working?

How might I Peter 3:7 be applied to the sharing of responsibilities between a husband and wife?

Please comment on Ecclesiastes 4:9-12 as it relates to both husband and wife working.

It appears that Lydia worked and was part of a household as well (Acts 16:11-15). She was a dealer of cloth (a retailer?), and was certainly in the marketplace in a traditional sense. Yet, the Bible is complementary about her openness to the message of Christ. She responded to the message by offering to open her home to Paul and his followers.

I Peter 3:7 says, "Husbands, in the same way be considerate as you live with your wives, and treat them with respect as the weaker partner and as heirs with you of the gracious gift of life, so that nothing will hinder your prayers." A minister we know says that many of the problems that crop up when both husband and wife work relate to the husband's unwillingness to shoulder his share of the burdens at home.

Discussion Questions

1. What special problems are created when both husband and wife work? What special benefits, other than financial, can come from both partners working?

2. How do you think working couples cope with the problems that arise from both working? What role would their Christian beliefs play?

3. What can men whose wives work do to help ease the tensions that can arise from the dual-income situation?

4. If you had a daughter who was married and had two preschool children, how would you advise her on whether or not she should work? What are the important questions you would ask? What are the key issues to be considered?

____

____

____

____

____

____

5. What can the local church do to help couples that work? What about assistance in providing support systems like day care and preschool? Other programs? Emotional support?

____

____

____

6. What guidance does the Bible offer on whether or not both husband and wife should work? How should they function, according to the Scriptures?

____

____

____

____

____

7

CHANGING JOBS OR CAREERS

Twentieth Century Americans, more than any other people in the history of the world, have the freedom and opportunity to change jobs or careers at almost any point in their lives. This is especially true for older Americans who find themselves relatively free from family obligations such as paying for college or helping their children in other ways. Early retirement programs abound, and more and more individuals in their early 50's are taking advantage of early retirement in order to begin second careers. Even those who reach 65 and are eligible for Social Security and other pension programs often use their new-found freedom from financial worries and family obligations to begin a new business or career.

Dr. Kenneth Dychtwald, a well-known gerontologist, says that in the future many individuals will have had two, three, and sometimes four or more careers during their lifetimes. A primary reason for this is a slowing down of the aging process; in other words, Americans are coming into their "retirement years" in excellent health with lots of energy. It is not uncommon for college classes to have 60- and 70-year-old men and women taking courses on a variety of subjects. Dychtwald says that the notion people should retire at age 65 goes back to pre-World War I Germany when most men were physically worn out at that age and typically had a remaining life expectancy of only two or three years.

During the course of a forty-year work career most people occasionally think about doing something else. Some of this is a longing for change due to boredom with doing the same old job for many years. In many cases family considerations, job security, and retirement plan vesting schedules make such changes impractical, or at least terribly difficult. But with the early vesting of many pension and profit sharing programs, and with the ability of many families to accumulate financial resources through IRA accounts, increased equity in homes, money market accounts, certificates of deposit, and stocks and bonds, the possibility of major career changes becomes more feasible.

Not all of the motivation for career changes is caused by a desire to take on a new challenge or simply to do something different. In our rapidly changing economy, human skills obsolescence is every bit as common as its technological counterpart. It is difficult in most industries to continue to perform the same job for 30 or 40 years; retraining has become increasingly common. Several of the heavily industrialized Midwestern states have been severely affected by job losses (the automobile and steel industries have been especially hard hit), and large numbers of older workers have had to learn new skills, be unemployed, or retire.

Burnout is another factor pushing people toward new and different careers. Some of the new jobs people take on are attempts to reduce stress or mitigate physical or emotional problems. One friend of ours who was the administrator of a large Christian ministry had to quit his job for health reasons (he was 59 at the time). He is now very happy driving a delivery van for an office supply company.

Over the years, numerous Christian pastors and speakers have challenged us to find a discussion of retirement in the Bible. The Scriptural concept of the body of Christ is that each person, regardless of age, is an important building block, or stone, holding the body together and ministering to it.

The issue for many of us is to find new areas of service, not only in the local fellowship, but in the world. And, to an extent unknown by our parents or grandparents, the opportunities come in many shapes and sizes. How do we decide when to make one of these life-changing shifts in our occupations? What factors do we, or should we, consider in these important decisions?

Snapshots from the Present

Scott, a banker, gave up a job with a California bank where he supervised 50 people, to move to another state for a lower paying job with less management responsibility. He said, "I wasn't a Christian at the time and I can't tell you why I decided to change jobs. But I'm glad I did because when we moved here we started attending church and I accepted Christ." Scott said that while he did not pray about his career change, his wife had been praying for 10 years for him to accept Christ as his Savior. "It took a major move to get me out of the rut I was in. The people I worked with in California thought I was crazy. Not a single person thought the move made any sense."

In looking ahead, Scott said that if it weren't for family financial needs, he would like to own and run a small retail business. "In all seriousness, I would rather run a hot dog stand than be a banker. But I have a family facing the need for financial support for their college educations. It would be irresponsible for me to consider a change now."

Don recently made a major career move, giving up his life insurance and financial services practice with a large international firm. He started a company to manufacture and market automatic testing equipment. Don, who became a Christian in 1976, served on his church's board of deacons from 1978 to 1984. "When my wife and I came off the board, we were looking for ways to serve. My original idea was to establish a labor-intensive assembly operation in a third-world country. As we began to look at various opportunities, we came across this unique piece of equipment that had been designed in England. As I began to check it out, I felt that here was a terrific opportunity placed before us by the Lord."

Don is now totally involved in his start-up company. "Although what we are doing today differs from our earlier concept back in 1985, it was our desire to serve God that led to this opportunity. If our new company is successful, my wife and I feel that it will open up countless additional opportunities to share financially and to provide new jobs in our community. We feel that this company is a Christian ministry."

Al began his career as a high school teacher. "But," he said, "I looked around at my large family and asked myself how I was going to feed them on the salary I was making. This led me into college administrative and fund-raising jobs for several different nonprofit organizations. In looking back, these job changes were easy; life just sort of unfolded naturally."

Over the past year Al and his family decided to give up a higher-paying job with a major medical center to work for a small Christian college. "When we started considering this change, it seemed like the Lord increased my desire to work for a small organization. We spent about three months in intensive prayer before finally making the move. So far we have been happy with the results."

Julie made a deliberate move from Virginia to Colorado following her divorce in 1978. "I really tried to make this decision in the right way. I prayed a lot. I systematically analyzed each alternative, including developing criteria and assigning points to each one. One important factor was the availability of an evangelical church. I also needed a teaching job where I earned a certain amount of money. Another criterion was that my home, job, and church all be within 15 minutes driving time of each other. I really felt the Lord's presence when I considered this move, and things worked out perfectly. I'm convinced I am where the Lord wants me."

One of the group members closed the discussion on career and job changes by observing that all of us are continuously assessing our job situations and available opportunities. He said, "I have a strong desire to make my life really count for the Lord; we all do. Therefore, there is a restlessness that many of us experience. Is this good or bad? Maybe we should be more content with what we have; I thank God for my job. Yet, I feel that somewhere out there the Lord has something else in mind for me. I'm looking forward to finding out what it is."

Snapshot from the Past:
Barnabas Changed Jobs (Acts 13—15)

Joseph, a Levite from Cyprus, was renamed Barnabas (Son of Encouragement) by the apostles. Barnabas not only changed jobs, but his name was changed as well.

Initially, Barnabas was the recognized leader of the Antioch church. He was involved in its early evangelism and growth. He recruited Saul (later called Paul) to help establish and disciple the Antioch congregation. Barnabas and Saul spent a whole year working together with these people.

Barnabas and Saul were commissioned by the church at Antioch for missionary work. At the start, Barnabas was the leader of the missionary team on Cyprus.

However, there was a "job change" on that first missionary trip. Saul (Paul) took over as leader. Until then it was "Barnabas and Saul," but now it was "Paul and Barnabas." Barnabas lost his job as leader of the missionary team. In fact, the leadership focus turned completely to Paul and his missionary companions.

Although later there was a sharp disagreement between Barnabas and Paul concerning John Mark, Barnabas was gracious and generous concerning his "lost job." To him, the job change was okay. He knew God had a purpose for him, so he apparently felt no bitterness toward Paul.

What attitudes did Barnabas likely possess that helped him through a difficult job change?

Scripture and Personal Application

The writer of Ecclesiastes notes that there is nothing better for people than to be happy and do good and to find satisfaction in their work (Eccl. 3:9-13). Note that in these verses the Bible talks about both satisfaction and the "burden" of providing for our needs. Do you think that workers in the U. S. today tend to be too restless, too dissatisfied? Explain or illustrate your response.

The Psalmist says, "Search me, O God, and know my heart; test me and know my anxious thoughts. See if there is any offensive way in me, and lead me in the way everlasting" (Ps. 139:23, 24). Thinking about changing careers or jobs can produce quite a bit of anxiety. How does this prayer apply to a career or job change?

"Do not wear yourself out to get rich; have the wisdom to show restraint" (Prov. 23:4). How do we balance our desires to make more money and move up the career ladder with the thrust of this passage?

____

____

____

____

Does Luke 9:62 relate to the matter of job changing? If so, how? If not, why not?

____

____

____

____

Writing in *Discipleship Journal* (No. 45, 1988), Marlowe Embree notes that there is no shortage of written material for the individual considering the change of a job or career. However, Embree laments the fact that most of what is available approaches the subject from a secular perspective. He suggests that a Christian should approach a job change by considering three principles: servanthood, stewardship, and calling.

The model of servanthood leads us to ask, "What needs do I see in my world?" The model of stewardship suggests the question, "What gifts and abilities do I have to meet these needs?" The model of calling provokes the inquiry, "Which particular combination of needs and gifts do I feel compelled to pursue?"

Embree says that together these three questions provide a useful context for every believer to examine his or her own career plans, goals, and choices. Scripture cited by Embree includes Romans 8:32; I Corinthians

12:18; and II Peter 1:3. Relate these passages and Embree's questions above to a job change you might contemplate.

Discussion Questions

1. What experience have you had in making a major career or job change? What factors motivated this change or changes?

2. Whom did you talk with or seek out for counsel? If you are married, what role did your spouse play in the decision? How valuable was this counsel? How much weight did you give it?

3. What role did prayer play in your decision? How did you sense the leading of the Holy Spirit? What difference does being a Christian make when you consider a major job or career change?

4. When a job or career change involves a move into full-time Christian service, are there special considerations over and above those faced with secular job changes? If so, what are they?

5. Do you know Christians who seem to be continually dissatisfied with their jobs? What would you say to such people if they were to ask your advice?

8

DEALING WITH UNEMPLOYMENT

Nothing is as threatening to most working people as the prospect of losing a job. Many individuals dread the time and effort—and the inevitable rejections—that come with job hunting. Yet, we live in a society in which job security is becoming increasingly rare. Organizations that seemed to be financially solid, with long records of successful service to the public, have run into financial difficulties leading to massive layoffs, bankruptcy, and closure.

The editors of *Forbes,* August 22, 1988, offered this observation on being unemployed:

> *The man out of work feels that the world is getting along very well without him. He is useless, superfluous, needed by no one, a nuisance. Nobody wants to hear his tale of woe. Everybody seems so busy with his own affairs, so preoccupied, so self-centered and so selfish. To be an outcast in the labor market first challenges and then often kills pride, confidence, and self-respect.*

Being a Christian is no guarantee of employment security. Many of us have faced the loss of a job, tried to help friends who are in that situation, or observed the mental anguish and hardship brought on by unemployment.

Snapshots from the Present

When Christians are struck by job losses, do they have special resources to enable them to face what can be personally and professionally devastating? Here are three case studies of Christians who were, at the time this book was prepared, looking for permanent employment.

George, 40 years old with six children aged 5 to 14, is an accountant. Although he has a degree in accounting, George has not yet qualified for his CPA certificate. George's most recent job was with an oil and gas firm; his last task was to liquidate the firm. That was four months ago.

Since then George has taken a variety of part-time jobs, including delivering pizza six nights a week. By doing this, George has been able to meet mortgage payments, but he has fallen behind on other obligations. His church has provided financial assistance.

George says that he went through a phase of "being mad at God." Now, however, he notes that the experiences of the past four months have drawn him closer to the Lord. George said, "I hope that my dependence on Him is as great when I find a job as it is now."

Peter, a 35-year-old geologist (with BS and MS degrees), was on a fast track with a major oil company. Then, eight months ago, disaster struck. Peter and many other geologists in his company were laid off.

Peter has three children under six, and his wife is expecting again in five months. They lost their house and have been "house sitting" for the past four months in a variety of homes that are on the market. Peter has had sporadic minimum wage jobs, and his wife worked up until a month ago. Their church and other Christian organizations have provided food and some money.

Peter says he will move *anywhere* for a job. He feels confident that he will find an excellent job and resume his professional career. He says that he and his wife have been through so many hardships that they have complete trust in God. "Without the Lord," Peter acknowledges, "we could not have survived."

Dave's career as a construction engineer began to run into problems three years ago. His company closed its Denver office, and he worked in the securities business for a year before resigning his $50,000 a year job. The past two years he has had several part-time and evening jobs; his wife has continued to work as a secretary.

By reducing their standard of living, Dave and his family (including two teenagers) have been able to meet mortgage payments.

Dave, at age 43, concedes that he may never have another permanent job paying as well as his previous positions. But, he says, "I can accept part-time or low-paying jobs knowing that they may be God's will at this time." Dave says he has gone through extreme emotional peaks and valleys, but he now feels peace about his circumstances.

A common theme of these three cases is that adversity brought the three individuals and their families closer to Christ. Without their Christian faith, all three say they would have been unable to survive the harsh difficulties they faced. All three have learned to take the Lord very seriously. This is their testimony.

These case studies illustrate how three Christians handled the loss of their jobs. How might they have reacted if they had not been Christians?

Snapshot from the Past:
Joseph Lost His Job (Genesis 37—50)

Joseph was the eleventh son of Jacob but the first son of Rachel, Jacob's favorite wife. Jacob was partial to Joseph, giving him special attention and the gift of his favorite coat. His favoritism made Joseph's brothers jealous, and their antagonism grew when Joseph told them they would one day bow down before him.

Eventually, Joseph's brothers sold him as a slave to a company of Ishmaelite merchants who took him to

Egypt. His brothers lied to their father, Jacob, telling him that Joseph had been killed by a wild beast.

In Egypt, Joseph was sold to Potiphar, the captain of Pharaoh's guard. As a trustworthy worker, Joseph was given a responsible position. However, Potiphar's wife was attracted to Joseph and attempted to seduce him. When Joseph declined her advances, she gave a false report that resulted in Joseph's imprisonment.

After several years in prison, Joseph was released when he accurately interpreted the pharaoh's dream. He then became the superintendent of the royal granaries, second in command to the pharaoh. Later, during a famine, Joseph met his family again.

Joseph experienced job losses. He was a wealthy and favored son, a slave, and then a prisoner before he became a prime minister. Joseph's exemplary character showed itself throughout the story. He was gentle, moral, patient, and consistent—even when he went through crushing job changes.

The Biblical account ends with Joseph's statement to his brothers, "You intended to harm me, but God intended it for good" (Gen. 50:20).

Scripture and Personal Application

One of the major results of being unemployed is the need to be dependent upon others in the local fellowship. Galatians 6:2-4 says, "Carry each other's burdens, and in this way you will fulfill the law of Christ. If anyone thinks he is something when he is nothing, he deceives himself. Each one should test his own actions. Then he can take pride in himself, without comparing himself to somebody else. . . ."

Another serious problem of being unemployed is the possible loss of self-esteem. The Bible has much to say about how valuable we are in God's sight. For example, read Ephesians 2:1-10. How does this passage speak to the question of self-esteem?

What other passages can you recall that describe God's esteem for us?

Philippians 4:4-7 tells us not to be anxious about anything, and that the peace of God will guard our hearts and minds. Paul goes on to say that, "I have learned the secret of being content in any and every situation, whether well-fed or hungry, whether living in plenty or in want" (Phil. 4:12). How do these verses apply to the question of self-esteem?

"Trust in the Lord with all your heart and lean not on your own understanding; in all your ways acknowledge him, and he will make your paths straight" (Prov. 3:5, 6). How do these promises speak to you or a friend who has lost a job?

Read Psalm 40 from the point of view of one who has just lost a job. In what ways could this chapter be encouraging during a period of unemployment?

Read Matthew 6:25-34. Write down your thoughts from

these verses, relating them to the situation of being unemployed.

Discussion Questions

1. Although not mentioned in the case studies, it is a fact that all three men relied on their network of friends and acquaintances in their churches for help. Is this a proper thing to do? If so, how can a person who is out of work benefit from such networking?

2. Is it proper for Christians who are out of work to lower their career expectations? George and Peter continue to have high expectations, whereas Dave indicates that he has accepted his fate. Which is the better outlook? Why?

3. What, if anything, can you do to prepare yourself for the possibility of future unemployment? Peter says that his father advised him to work for a large company for job security. Dave says just the opposite; he believes that those who own their own businesses have the most control. In your opinion, who is right?

9

DEALING WITH OTHER CHRISTIANS

"Some of the dealings I've had with Christians have been among the worst experiences I have ever had in my business career," said one focus group participant. "I get the feeling that some Christians look for ways to take advantage of their brothers and sisters in Christ, possibly on the assumption that we are pushovers."

What about doing business with Christians? Are there special precautions that we need to take? Should we go out of our way to do business with Christians, or to employ Christians who need work, in order to help further the Kingdom of God?

Snapshots from the Present

Jan and her husband run a large Christian bookstore in Pennsylvania. She says, "By and large, Christians are wonderful to work with and to serve as customers. However, we do have a few individuals, including some pastors, who seem to want to take advantage of us. Maybe they are naive. Anyway, these people come in and ask for free books or other materials for use in some 'very worthwhile ministry with people who can't afford to pay.' They don't seem to realize that our suppliers demand payment from us; suppliers don't know, or care, whether we sell the material or give it away, as long as they get paid. We hear lots of sob stories, and I'm sure that many of them are valid, but we can't stay in business if we continually give away our products."

Jan went on to point out some other aspects of doing business with church workers and staff. "Many of them are very careless about violating the copyright laws. They don't realize that it is the same as stealing to copy music or other materials in order to avoid purchasing extra copies. Also, there is a tendency to trade quality for lower priced merchandise; many churches are willing to accept second- or third-rate materials. And lots of our customers expect discounts just because they are Christians or are purchasing something for a Bible study, Sunday school, or other organized religious activity." She pointed out one other annoyance of being in business: constant solicitation by charitable organizations for money or free merchandise. Some people get very upset when we turn them down."

John sums up his experience in dealing with Christians by saying, "Christians are people. If I expected that my Christian clientele were any different from my other clients, I would be in for a surprise. Some Christians don't pay their bills, and some try to take advantage of us, but the majority are great people, just like a cross section of the people who live in our area."

Bill and his wife have operated a large plant nursery for 17 years. "As I look back, I realize that both my best and worst experiences were with Christians. I'll never forget when we first started, and were hungry for business, that a member of our church gave us complete freedom in deciding how to landscape his yard. He trusted us to do the job right and not overcharge him. It was an important vote of confidence for us at that time. But in another instance, several years later, another member of our church had us do a substantial amount of landscaping and then never paid us a dime. I guess he figured he needed the money worse than we did!"

Bill brought up the question of whether to advertise in the so-called Christian Yellow Pages. "I remember, a few years ago, when these listings came out. I thought about it and then refused to advertise in them. I wanted to be known as a Christian business owner, but I didn't feel right about advertising that fact. The people soliciting my account didn't seem to understand my reasoning."

Bill said that he goes out of his way to do business with others who he knows are Christians. "I don't do it because I expect something in return; I just feel that I want to help those who are trying to glorify God with their businesses."

Sandra is an interior decorator, and a large percentage of her customers are Christians. She said her experiences have typically been excellent. However, she related a recent experience that involved employing a part-time pastor who worked as a carpenter. "The first time I used this man, he showed up three hours late. My client wasn't pleased, but she didn't say much. Then, the next day he came two hours late. This aggravated my client and she expressed her displeasure. This man is young and I wonder if I should tell him how his performance is adversely affecting his witness."

Phil has his own real estate company and works with both Christian and non-Christian customers. "The thing that puts me on guard is the person who comes right out and says, 'I am a Christian.' I haven't had many positive experiences with people who flaunt their Christianity. When I'm screening potential renters or buyers, I am looking for people of good character. I can pick that up from the way they talk and conduct themselves." Another member of the group concurred that he is suspicious of potential clients who are aggressive in terms of their Christian beliefs. He said, "Some of the biggest con artists I've dealt with come across as holier-than-thou Christians. Our actions and life-styles speak louder than our words. They don't seem to realize that."

Tom shared about a current situation he faces in dealing with a Christian company. "I have been helping these folks with some exciting new computer applications. Up until now I haven't charged them anything, but a couple of months ago one computer application emerged that could have wide-ranging financial implications for them and for me. A friend advised me that it was time to formalize our relationship, and I agreed. I asked the head of this firm to draft an agreement. He said he would, but that was two months ago and I haven't seen or heard anything. It bothers me that he apparently doesn't think it is very important."

Major Issues

One of the issues discussed by the group was the kind of expectations we should have when dealing with a Christian as an employee, supplier, or customer. One person said, "I can't help but have higher expectations when I'm dealing with believers. I know, from hard experience, that I'm setting myself up for a letdown when I do that. But I keep hoping." Others simply view Christians as regular people and don't expect higher ethical or work standards. This issue seems to revolve around where Christians are in terms of their spiritual growth or maturity and how prevalent the fruits of the Spirit are in their lives.

There was nearly unanimous agreement among the focus group participants that Christians should have written contracts when entering into business arrangements among themselves. Putting the terms of an agreement in writing is more businesslike, and it helps prevent later disagreements or differing interpretations of who is to do what. Several individuals cited personal cases in which they failed to execute a written agreement, and noted the unnecessary problems and hard feelings that often resulted.

One person, who is in the oil and gas business, pointed out that this industry has traditionally operated on the basis of a handshake, and the system has served the industry very well. "Those individuals or companies who take advantage of the system aren't invited to participate in deals in the future; this essentially takes them out of the business."

There was a consensus that Christians should not sue other Christians. Disagreements and conflicts should be resolved in other ways. One member of the group added, "I don't think the Bible precludes us from suing non-Christians if the need arises."

There were differences of opinion on the issue of whether to have non-Christian business partners. One individual, who is in partnership with two other Christians, said, "I believe the Bible teaches that we should not be unequally yoked with unbelievers." Larry Burkett, well-known lecturer on Christians in business, takes a strong position on this issue. Based on his experience, he believes that such a business association (mix of Christians and others) will eventually fail. One of the authors has had a different experience, having been in partnership with non-Christians, Jews and others, for 17 years. A supporter of this position said, "I don't believe that Christ taught us to isolate ourselves from the world. If we are going to have an impact, and have opportunities to witness, we need to be rubbing elbows with people of all types. We can't live in the ivory tower of Christianity and still be the salt of the earth."

Should Christians who borrow money from other Christians pay interest on the loan? This is an intriguing question when the borrowing party is in dire financial straights and the loan is based more on heartfelt compassion than on an objective analysis of the person's ability to repay. Some individuals advise that when we desire to make this type of loan, we should view it as a donation and not expect to receive interest or repayment. Otherwise we should withhold the funds.

Christians who own or manage businesses are frequently asked to donate funds, goods, or services to Christian organizations. Owners want to be fair and equitable with the wide variety of Christian groups seeking support, while at the same time wanting to avoid being taken advantage of. One person said, "Once you start supporting these various groups, and I'm including community organizations, they drive you crazy with requests, especially over the phone. It is not much fun telling them that you can't help, and sometimes they aren't very understanding."

Snapshot from the Past:
Solomon and Hiram (I Ki. 5, 9; II Chron. 2)

King Solomon of Israel and King Hiram of Phenicia did business with each other. Solomon and Hiram used the barter system by exchanging products and services.

Solomon needed wood, gold, and craftsmen in various trades to assume the task of building the Temple in Jerusalem. In exchange for wood and skilled labor Solomon furnished Hiram with agricultural products such as wheat, barley, wine, and oil. For the gold, Solomon gave Hiram a tract of land in Galilee which encompassed 20 towns. When he saw this district, however, Hiram was quite unhappy and displeased. In spite of this, Solomon and Hiram's good business relationship of over 20 years continued unbroken.

Having established a good business agreement for building purposes, Solomon and Hiram also drew up a business contract for a joint commercial endeavor. Hiram and Solomon successfully built a navy and supplied it with seamen. Once again, they shared profitable trade with each other.

Solomon and Hiram were able to conduct business with each other satisfactorily over a long period of time. Although there was a potential conflict at one point, they apparently resolved it.

How could you work out a problem with a business associate using Solomon and Hiram's example?

Scripture and Personal Application

One of the most frequently cited passages on the issue of working with non-believers is II Corinthians 6:14-16. "Do not be yoked together with unbelievers. For what do righteousness and wickedness have in common? Or what fellowship can light have with darkness? What harmony is there between Christ and Belial? What does a believer have in common with an unbeliever? What agreement is there between the temple of God and idols? For we are the temple of the living God. . . ."

Does this passage mean that Christians should have no business partnerships with non-Christians? If so, how does this view relate to the need for Christians to be in the world where they can be witnesses?

Deuteronomy 22:10 says, "Do not plow with an ox and a donkey yoked together." Amos 3:3 asks, "Do two walk together unless they have agreed to do so?" Can a Christian, living through the power of the Holy Spirit, walk in business with a non-believer? Amplify your view.

Read I Corinthians 6:1-8. Doing business with other believers sometimes resulted in problems in the early church. Galatians 6:10 says, "Therefore, as we have opportunity, let us do good to all people, especially to those who belong to the family of believers." How does this relate to doing business with other Christians?

Read Ecclesiastes 4:9-12. How does this relate to working with Christians?

Does Proverbs 17:17 impose a responsibility on Christians? What kind? What are some typical problems one will face when trying to implement this verse?

Discussion Questions

1. What personal experiences have you had in dealing with Christians in business? Positive? Negative? How have your experiences compared with your expectations?

2. What are your feelings about using church members as sales prospects? Do you like being approached by a fellow church member who is soliciting your business?

3. Should you go out of your way to patronize businesses owned or managed by Christians? Under what conditions? When you do so, do you expect a discount or other special considerations?

4. What is the appropriate response when a Christian supplier of goods or services fails to deliver in a satisfactory manner? Have you had this happen? What did you do about it? What were the results?

5. Tell about a successful business venture that you had with another person. Explain what made it successful.

10

ETHICAL QUESTIONS

A recent article in *Time* magazine started with "Ethics, often dismissed as a prissy Sunday School word, is now at the center of a new national debate." According to Webster, ethics is the study of standards of conduct and moral judgment. Christians in business have the Bible as their "standard of conduct," but is it being applied appropriately in an increasingly competitive and complex business environment?

Another *Time* article caught our eye, "Publish or Perish or Fake It". This June 8, 1987 issue deals with a medical researcher who falsified his research findings. Describing the current academic environment, *Time* uses words that sound similar to those bandied about in the business world. "The competition is savage. Winners reap monumental rewards; losers face oblivion. It's an atmosphere in which an illicit shortcut is sometimes irresistible—not least because the Establishment is frequently squeamish about confronting wrongdoing."

The *Wall Street Journal* reported in its October 10, 1987 edition that ethical lapses in business, especially in large corporations, are becoming increasingly common. After reviewing 10 different academic studies on ethics in business, the *Journal* said: "The studies together indicate that even the most upright people are apt to become dishonest and unmindful of their civic responsibilities when placed in a typical corporate environment."

All of this sounds ominous, but what are some of the typical kinds of ethical issues faced by a Christian in business or at work? Do Christians have any safeguards available that make them less susceptible to the kinds of situations described above?

Most ethical issues differ, in our judgment, from questions of honesty. Making copies of copyrighted material is dishonest. Cheating on an expense account is stealing from an employer or client. There are no great ethical issues involved in these kinds of run-of-the-mill acts that go on in thousands of businesses every day. Christians shouldn't even consider participating in such illicit activities. But there are other less clearly defined ethical issues with which Christians will struggle.

Snapshots from the Present

Frank, a financial planner, said that, "Greed is at the root of most ethical breakdowns. The company I worked with for many years has shifted to a strictly bottom-line approach with less attention to quality. This leaves me cold. They have every right to make this shift; they own the company. There is nothing illegal; it is simply a matter of priorities."

Al said, "I've always respected people who keep their word, even when it involves insignificant matters or small details. I used to have a boss who did absolutely everything he said he would do; he never had a lapse. If he said he would call someone on a certain date, he would do it—without fail. I think that carelessness in our commitments can represent a breach of ethics. It seems to me that people who are absolutely dependable are in very short supply these days."

Bill talked about oil companies leasing land from farmers. "When we negotiate a lease, we often know more than the landowner about what is under the ground and what is planned in the way of drilling in the area. And, we know the going market value for leases. An unethical landsman can take advantage of the situation and negotiate a lease far below market value. This isn't dishonest, but it is certainly unethical. Fortunately, it doesn't happen too often, but the opportunity exists."

Greg told of a case where he had advanced notification of a planned interstate highway route. This information was to be held in strict confidence until publicly released. During this waiting period, Greg learned that farm land located on the designated corridor was for sale. "I could have bought a large block of this land for $200 an acre. After the announcement, the land would have jumped immediately to over $1,000 per acre. My finding out about the land being available was a coincidence, but it wouldn't have looked that way to the public. Naturally, I didn't do it."

Mark, who works for a large corporation, noted that in bidding for certain large contracts, information sometimes leaks out about the customer's budget or about what competitors are likely to bid. "Sharing price information with competitors violates antitrust laws; you can go to jail for that sort of behavior. But, there are cases where valuable information comes into our hands that could give us a competitive advantage. When this happens, there is always a question of what to do."

The treatment of employees can also raise ethical issues, according to Mark. "What are fair pay standards? And, are fringe benefits what they should be? Are we making additional profits by penalizing our employees?" Another area of concern is the sale and distribution of products that may not perform as advertised. In some cases, there are real questions about product performance. "It's a gray area," Mark said.

John noted that a number of ethical issues surface in the practice of medicine. "There are numerous opportunities to cheat a patient in terms of the procedures or medicines used. A young physician, trying to establish his or her practice, may be tempted to perform certain medical procedures that could be better accomplished by a specialist (for example, a family practitioner deciding to interpret X-rays and set broken bones)."

Ted, a political scientist and consultant with many years' experience in Washington, D.C., noted several examples of questionable ethics in decision-making within the Federal Government. "The special interest groups in this country have gotten out of control. Is it proper to maintain an obsolete military base in a community just to preserve jobs in that area? The tobacco industry has, for years, successfully resisted efforts to present the truth about what tobacco does to the human body; we even subsidize farmers who grow the stuff! Facts in research reports are distorted to prove a point. Information that could be valuable to another person is withheld. The list goes on and on. What really gets to me is that we have gotten so used to this sort of thing that it doesn't seem to bother us any more."

A friend of one of the authors recently told him of an ethical dilemma he faces relative to his boss. "My boss and his secretary are very close; they have lunch together nearly every day, and she spends a lot of time in his office. She obviously takes advantage of the situation, coming in late for work or taking off when she shouldn't. This has been going on for two years. My boss's supervisor is so busy he doesn't know what is going on in our shop. I know it isn't right, and maybe I should say something to either my boss or his supervisor. Of course, by blowing the whistle, I risk losing my job. In the meantime, our company is being ripped off."

Snapshot from the Past: Daniel Faced Compromise (Dan. 1)

Would Old Testament Daniel compromise in a job setting? If so, how and why? What were his convictions? Where did he "draw the line"? Daniel faced hard ethical questions at his work.

Daniel and others were taken captive by Nebuchadnezzar from religious Jerusalem to secular Babylon. Because of his fine appearance and abilities, Daniel, along with others, was selected for training to work in the king's court. Daniel was instructed for three years in the customs and language of the pagan Chaldeans. He was also given the Babylonian name of Belteshazzar.

Daniel attended the pagan schools, learned the language, and received the name the Chaldeans gave him. There was no problem here. However, despite his conformity to much of the Babylonian system, Daniel declined to partake of their royal food and drink. He "drew the line" here because this violated his convictions concerning God's dietary laws. The food in question was also tainted through ceremonial contact with idols.

At their request, Daniel and his friends were allowed to eat only vegetables and drink water. As a result they were in better health than the other trainees. The supervisors observed this and concluded that these Jewish youths possessed great skill and wisdom.

Daniel faced ethical questions wisely. He willingly embraced some job standards but graciously declined others that violated his conscience and convictions before God.

Daniel was fully convinced that he wanted to do God's will. We have no indication that his commitment to God ever wavered. How would you describe your own level of commitment at this point in your life?

Scripture and Personal Application

Proverbs 24:26 says, "An honest answer is like a kiss on the lips." What does this mean within this discussion of marketplace ethics?

"Do not pervert justice or show partiality. Do not accept a bribe, for a bribe blinds the eyes of the wise and twists the words of the righteous" (Deut.16:19). What sorts of "bribes" are you faced with?

Does Proverbs 6:16-19 have anything to do with ethics? Explain.

"If a person sins because he does not speak up when he hears a public charge to testify regarding something he has seen or learned about, he will be held responsible" (Lev. 5:1; please also see Deut. 1:17 and Prov. 21:3). How might this warning apply to you when you face ethical questions on the job?

In his testimony before Felix, Paul said, "So I strive always to keep my conscience clear before God and man" (Acts 24:16). What was Paul's "conscience" based upon?

Read Deuteronomy 25:13-16. How does this warning affect you and your work?

Please read Proverbs 11:1; 16:11 and 20:10. Why so much emphasis on weights and scales? How does this apply today?

Discussion Questions

1. What are some examples of ethical decisions, or issues, in your work?

2. What do you look for when evaluating the ethics of people you work with: fellow employees, suppliers, customers? Are there any clues that we should look for?

3. There is a tendency for many people to blame others for their problems or for adverse circumstances. When problems occur they often blame someone else. Have you ever seen this sort of "passing the buck"—avoiding responsibility for one's own actions? How does this relate to our discussion of ethics?

____

____

____

____

4. Karen Moy, a systems analyst with an insurance company, offered these reactions to playing office politics. "My experience has been that in the business world, honesty and sheer hard work will eventually get you farther than any amount of games-playing. After all, God is a *rational* God. I don't think He selected honesty as a virtue for arbitrary reasons. He did it because it *works.* Even in the marketplace. . . . Now, does this mean you should sit passively by and await the outcome? Certainly not! So many of the college students I've talked with seem to think that as Christians in the marketplace they'll automatically come out on the short end of the political stick—that their ethical standards will prevent them from being 'winners.' Well, it doesn't work that way. Good guys and gals *do* win sometimes. Many times, in fact." This quote is from *Marketplace Networks,* January, 1988. What is your reaction to this philosophy of the payoff from ethical business practices?

____

____

____

____

____

5. Can you be guilty of unethical behavior by *not* taking action? For example, is it unethical for a business to withhold support from certain important community services, like United Way? Should your organization be looking for opportunities to employ mentally or physically handicapped individuals? We know there are sins of omission; does the same apply for business ethics? Examples?

6. Have you ever taken a stand on an ethical issue in your business or where you work? Please describe the situation and what you did about it.

7. Describe the most ethical person you have ever worked with or been associated with in business. Was Christianity a part of this person's ethical standards? If so, how did his or her spiritual values seem to influence behavior?

8. How do you decide when to "stick it out"—to try to correct a situation—or when to resign?

9. Is being ethical in business or at work "good for business"? In other words, based on your experience and observations, is ethical behavior rewarded?

11

FELLOWSHIP ON THE JOB

What is Christian fellowship? One focus group participant said it is the ability to share with another Christian without barriers. Another person emphasized that it is support for each other. "To me, Christian fellowship is the ability to approach problems from a different perspective—the perspective of Christ—with other Christians. It is hard to find this in business."

One member of the group said, "I don't think most Christians realize they need fellowship until they have experienced it. Then it can become very important. Once we have experienced it, we will find ways to satisfy this deep-seated need we all have."

The *Wall Street Journal,* December 1985, reported that there is a trend toward Christian workers getting together for fellowship and Bible study during the day. "At Seattle's Boeing Co., about 200 employees in a group called Good News at Work gather in corporate cafeterias for breakfast and lunchtime Bible studies and inspirational talks. In the Arizona desert, as many as 40 construction workers building the Palo Verde nuclear plant conduct daily lunchtime Bible studies at the work site."

This chapter talks about the various ways a Christian can have work or business-related fellowship with other Christians. The case studies represent a wide variety of experiences, mostly successful, on how to experience Christian fellowship in the marketplace.

Snapshots from the Present

Chuck, who works for a government agency as part of a group of 75 people, said, "I made up my mind three years ago that I wanted to find a Christian 'buddy' in my organization. I had in mind someone at my level who I could share with regularly in a meaningful way." He went on, "God answered my prayer; I found another Christian. I started by inviting him out for coffee and we clicked right from the beginning. We get together for a few minutes every day to share and sometimes to pray. We don't hold anything back from each other. It has been a wonderful relationship." Chuck added, "Not every one of our meetings centers on spiritual growth concerns. Many times we talk about rather mundane matters. But, when a problem comes up, we have a relationship and we can deal with the situation through prayer and sharing."

Greg had a different experience. "A few years ago some of my employees started a Bible study at work. It started off with a bang, and I attended the first two sessions. However, I started to hear some rumblings from both inside and outside city hall and I decided that I should not continue to participate. In my situation as city administrator, I have to be very careful not to show favoritism. I wasn't, but some people could have interpreted it that way." He went on, "The group continued for a few months and then gradually died out. I was kind of relieved."

Greg told about a young man, a Christian, who was with the organization for three years. He said, "Even though this person didn't work directly for me (there was a department head between us), we did work together very closely during the entire period. We seemed to have the ability to understand each other quickly.

Sometimes it didn't take a lot of words, but we could zero in on a problem and really understand it from a Christian perspective." Did the special relationship create any problems? "It probably would have if he hadn't been so capable. Also, we didn't really spend much time together. It was just that the time we had was extremely rewarding."

Since he has only been in his new job for less than six months, Greg doesn't have many Christian contacts within the firm. "However, I do get together for lunch once a month with two different fellows from our church. I enjoy this as a way to have fellowship during the week." When asked about the spiritual depth of the conversations, Greg said, "We visit more as two friends just getting together casually. But, I know if I needed to talk over a problem, we could do it and have a Christian perspective on the situation."

Al shared what it can be like to work for a Christian organization. "I came in one day last week and found that we had a severe financial problem. Working in the area of fund raising, I was naturally concerned about the problem; I could feel the pressure. I immediately called everyone in the department together for a time of prayer, and we soon felt the burden lifting. As we went on with our work that day we all had a sense of peace and had a tremendously productive day. I've never experienced anything like this in the other places I've worked."

Bill, who owns a nursery and employs about 50 people (many part-time), said that he does not want to start a Bible study at work. "About half my workers are Christians, including several who are seminary students. I don't want to give the appearance of pressuring my non-Christian employees. They know where I stand, and I try hard to be an example of a Christian businessman. If they want to talk about being a Christian, that's fine. Otherwise, I don't push it."

Ted said that until recently he has never had another man, or small group of men, that he could share deeply with. "There is a group of 7 or 8 of us who have been meeting together for several years. It has taken me a couple of years to get to the point where I can share things of a very personal nature. This is extremely valuable to me; I don't know now how I could survive without it. And it is interesting that, with a diverse group, suggestions and ways to pray for specific situations come from the least expected sources. The Holy Spirit is truly present with us."

Mark has a Christian secretary. "I don't know if I would say that we have fellowship, but it is certainly nice to have a Christian as a secretary. She is a perceptive person. Sometimes when she senses that I'm getting a little stressed out, I'll find clippings in my in-basket from one of Chuck Swindoll's books or a cartoon from *Christianity Today*. There is a noon Bible study at work, but I haven't participated."

Mark went on to tell about the relationship he had a few years ago with another member of the marketing staff of his firm. "When we were at sales meetings it was nice to be able to get together during the breaks or in the evening after the formal sessions were over. While most of the others were at the bar, we had some meaningful times together. In fact, at that stage in my Christian walk, those times really had an impact on me. As I look back, I'm grateful for this person and the time we spent together."

When one of the authors walked into Don's office for a 7:30 a.m. meeting, Don was having a Bible study with one of his associates. "It is nice to have colleagues who share my view that this is the Lord's company, particularly when we're up against a serious problem. We don't talk a lot about Christ during these crises, but we have an understanding that is unspoken." Don went on, "We are now moving into a mode of raising capital for our venture, and we are meeting with some high-powered people. It is great to be able to precede these presentations with prayer."

Tom said that his relationship with one of the people who works for him is special. "We don't have a Bible study or anything like that, but we have a great supportive relationship." He went on to say, "My boss is also a Christian. While we don't have a lot of fellowship, I find it helpful in terms of accountability; our fellowship keeps me on my toes."

Al told about getting together weekly with three other men whom he met while he was working on a Billy Graham Crusade. "None of us are in the same business, but this little group is becoming very, very important to me. One of the most important benefits to me is finding out that they have problems, too; I'm not the only one. They are struggling with the same things I am."

Other Issues

Reviewing the experiences of individuals in the group, we found that there were various levels of fellowship, from casual contacts to long-term, in-depth relationships with one individual. One person said that he had developed a close relationship with only one individual in his entire life. "It took us four years to develop this closeness, and then we moved to Denver. But, if my friend calls me, I'll get in the car and drive 1,000 miles to spend a few hours with him; that's how close we are even today."

Several individuals were aware of Bible studies or prayer groups of business people all over the metropolitan area. There is a strong network already established and it is relatively easy, with a few contacts, to tap into one of these groups. One person said, "There really isn't any excuse for someone who is working not to have fellowship with other Christians; it is going on all around us."

The group agreed that fellowship takes time. It is like everything else of value, including a marriage relationship. Time must be invested to develop or maintain a relationship. As we have seen, it sometimes takes months and years of meeting regularly to establish a deep and trusting relationship.

The authors have noted, in their experiences, that many business people make decisions without talking matters through with someone they can trust. In many cases, especially among men, we have no one to talk with whom we totally trust. As a result, we may make bad decisions that might have been avoided.

Snapshot from the Past:
Paul Needed Fellowship (Acts 17, 18)

Though he made tents to earn money, Paul's overarching calling, or job, was planting churches. He was an evangelist and a missionary. Wherever Paul traveled, he proclaimed Christ, established churches, and enlisted leaders.

However, Paul usually had fellowship on the job. Barnabas went with him on his first missionary journey. On his second journey Paul traveled with Silas from city to city, establishing churches.

In spite of strong opposition from the Jewish mobs, Paul and Silas experienced good results in Thessalonica and Berea. Finally, after intense pressure from a group of Jews, a few believers took Paul to distant Athens, leaving Silas and Timothy with the young Christians of the region.

At this point Paul was alone on the job in Athens. Although Paul preached hard in Athens, the results were minimal. Later Paul went to Corinth alone. He met and stayed with Aquila and Priscilla, but he seemed to miss the fellowship of his colleagues, Silas and Timothy. Seemingly Paul was weak, fearful, ineffective, and lonely. But his spirit lifted noticeably when Silas and Timothy joined him in Corinth (Acts 18:5). He became upbeat, positive, and committed. He now had Christian fellowship again on the job.

Scripture and Personal Application

Matthew 18:20 says, "For where two or three come together in my name, there am I with them." Christians in business often long for this kind of close fellowship and the power that comes with it. Read Acts 2:1, 42, 44-47. The passage gives us insight into the New Testament church and how it functioned in the days following Pentecost. The believers shared their possessions and distributed to fellow Christians as they had need. There was a singleness of heart and a life of praise for God. Do you think there was also fellowship in the marketplace and at work? Is it any wonder that Christians today long for a closer spiritual relationship with other Christians at work? What practical suggestions might bring this to pass in your work situation?

Hebrews 3:13 says that we should encourage one another daily or we may become hardened to sin. This is a very real possibility in today's marketplace. How does this verse speak to the *kind* of fellowship we need at work?

According to Galatians 6:2 we should "carry each others burdens, and in this way you will fulfill the law of Christ." The workplace has more than its share of problems and burdens; therefore, this passage must apply. Do you agree? If so, how can we do it?

Does Romans 14:13 apply to fellowship on the job? How far does our responsibility extend in this matter?

Proverbs 27:17 says, "As iron sharpens iron, so one man sharpens another." Many of us have found this to be true in all aspects of our lives, including our work. How do you apply this passage to your job?

The author of Hebrews reminds us, "And let us consider how we may spur one another on toward love and good deeds. Let us not give up meeting together, as some are in the habit of doing, but let us encourage one another—and all the more as you see the Day approaching" (Heb. 10:24, 25). Does this passage refer to meeting for worship, fellowship during the week, or both? What are some practical approaches you use to encourage others you work with?

"The way of the fool seems right to him, but a wise man listens to advice" (Prov. 12:15). How do you make use of this truth at work?

Read Philippians 2:1-4. How does this passage relate to your work?

Discussion Questions

1. How do you define Christian fellowship? How does your definition apply to business or the workplace?

2. Do you have opportunities for fellowship in your work? With fellow employees? Customers or clients? Describe the quality of that fellowship.

3. Is it wise to share confidential matters and concerns with other Christians with whom you work? Under what circumstances, or with what limitations? Is this sort of sharing potentially harmful to your career? Explain.

4. In your work situation, do you feel it is better to look outside your organization for opportunities for Christian fellowship? Explain your view.

5. How would you advise a new Christian to find ways to have fellowship on the job? How should he or she go about getting something going?

6. How does fellowship affect your attitude toward your work? What difference does it make?

7. Describe a time when you were without fellowship at work. How did it affect you? What steps did you take to find someone you could fellowship with?

12

WITNESSING AT WORK

One definition of witnessing is: being called upon to describe what you saw or talk about the truth in some event. One of the authors has appeared as an expert witness on more than 200 occasions. An expert witness has certain protections and the ability to rely on personal experience and professional knowledge. When all else fails, an expert witness can say, "Based on my experience, I believe that . . . ." The judge, jury, or hearing panel may disagree, but they cannot deny an expert witness the opportunity to express his or her opinion.

Don said, "We talked earlier about being bold. We don't have to wear a fish pin or have a bumper sticker on our car to be bold." He added, "We can be bold by giving God the glory when certain things happen in our businesses. We can be bold by offering to pray for people when they have needs they have shared with us. God wants us to be like salt, and we can't do that by being timid." He went on, "As Christians, we don't need to tell everything we know to the people we are witnessing to. We need to stick with the basics."

The group talked about two general types of witnessing at work. The first involves direct confrontation of fellow workers and others with the claims of the Gospel. The second is based on letting our actions speak louder than our words; it depends on how we conduct our business or how we handle ourselves in a work situation.

Snapshots from the Present

Frank cited a time when he witnessed to a Jewish employee in his firm. "It started out by my being friendly with him and then inviting him to have a Bible study with me right there in the office. It was low pressure. As we met, our friendship increased to the point where I was able to invite him to accept Christ. I was relaxed because I trusted the Holy Spirit to do the work; *I knew I wasn't responsible for the results*. Then he heard that I was going to a weekly Bible fellowship and indicated an interest in attending. He came with me several times, and I could see some real changes taking place in his life."

Chuck said that he makes a point of contacting new employees in his department. "I introduce myself and ask them a few questions about themselves. Then when I see them around the office, I know a little about them and can continue to build a relationship. One of the new secretaries was upset a few weeks ago, and I asked her about it. One of her children was quite ill, and I told her I would pray for her daughter. This seemed to have a major impact on this woman and built a further relationship between the two of us." Chuck went on, "I've found that you can't witness effectively to people 'cold'; you have to establish some kind of relationship in order to be effective."

John shared from his experience. "If a person is truly a Christian and turned on for the Lord, that individual is probably an excellent employee. This type of worker is probably not going to show up for work with a Bible in one hand and tracts in the other. He is going to be concentrating on the job while he is there. I did have a young lady, one of my best employees, who was really enthused about witnessing. She would leave a Bible on the table in the waiting room, and was certainly not shy about telling people about the Lord, but she was first of all attentive to her work."

Greg commented that "when you are in the public sector it is often hard to share your faith, or to let people know you are a Christian. I remember one time, several years ago, I suggested that the city council meetings be opened with prayer. I had one of the council members ready to lead, and he gave a nice, very general prayer; the meeting went well. However, that week I found myself in quite a political storm. It turned out that there were three Jewish women in the audience and they were offended by the prayer. I discussed it with the mayor, and we reluctantly agreed that we should not begin future meetings with prayer. I was disappointed, but those are the facts of life that you have to live with."

Greg also told about two businessmen in the downtown area who were very dynamic Christians. "They organized an early morning Bible study that went on for seven or eight years and led many other business people to the Lord. One of the individuals was content to present the Gospel and let the Holy Spirit do the work, but the other wanted to see results. He began pushing harder and harder. He started turning people off, and the group eventually disbanded."

Sandra said, "I think there are certain situations in which a Christian has a greater opportunity to share. One time I went to work as a waitress for a large hotel chain. We were supposed to dress a certain way, keep our fingernails at a certain length, and adhere to other fairly rigid requirements. But nobody did it. Since I was new and didn't know any better, I did everything by the rules. Because the management liked me and held me up as an example to the other waitresses, some of whom were quite young, I had many chances to talk with these gals and lots of opportunities to share Christ."

Comments and Observations

Referring to Greg's example of the two businessmen and their evangelizing techniques, we feel there is a real danger of crossing the line—becoming too aggressive and turning people off. On the other hand, most people are probably too timid. How do we find the right balance? Our personalities and specific circumstances have a lot to do with the way we work and witness. The pat answer is to say we should be sensitive to the leading of the Holy Spirit. But how do we do this, particularly as potential witnessing opportunities often come up unexpectedly?

One individual shared that every once in a while he is asked for his views on a controversial social or political issue. "When this happens, I try to inject my basic philosophy; that is, where I am coming from as I personally evaluate these issues. I try very hard not to get argumentative, because if that happens I've clouded the waters. Then it's harder for people to remember the point I'm trying to make: that I am a Christian and that this affects my viewpoint on life." Some of the issues that provide opportunities to witness include homosexuality, abortion, nuclear weapons and disarmament, the proper role of government, and various national economic policies.

Coach Ken Hatfield of the University of Arkansas football team was criticized, according to *Sports Illustrated* (Nov. 21, 1988) by Mr. Broyles, his athletic director, for being too aggressive in promoting his religious convictions. "Broyles also confronted Hatfield on a more sensitive issue. 'I told him that his emphasis on religion was divisive,' says Broyles. The message was clear: Hatfield, a devout fundamentalist, was to stop wearing his religion so publicly. Among other things, he is to refrain from opening his Sunday-afternoon TV show with a verse from the Scriptures." What would you do if you were in Coach Hatfield's position?

The group discussed the benefits and disadvantages of using "pre-packaged" witnessing approaches compared to encouraging individuals to develop their own approaches. The authors are of the opinion that Christians should have a well-thought out approach, and one that includes memorizing several relevant Scripture passages. What approach to witnessing do you find most comfortable and effective?

Snapshot from the Past: A Fiery Witness (Dan. 3)

King Nebuchadnezzar supervised the construction of a huge golden image and then invited the community leaders to come for its dedication. At the dedication service the king officially announced that all should bow down and worship the image every time they heard music. If anyone showed an unwillingness to worship the golden image, he would be thrown immediately into a blazing furnace.

Soon King Nebuchadnezzar received a report that three young Jewish men—Shadrach, Meshach, and Abednego—had ignored the king's mandate to worship the image. The king was furious, and he called the three Jewish men before him to verify the report. Furthermore, the king threatened them with being thrown into the fiery furnace and asked, "What god will be able to rescue you from my hand?" (Dan. 3:15).

Shadrach, Meshach, and Abednego replied to the king that the God (Yahweh) they served was able to save and deliver them from the hand of the king. The three went on to say that even if their God didn't save them, they would not serve other gods or worship the golden image.

King Nebuchadnezzar's anger was piqued as he heard the strong witness of Shadrach, Meshach, and Abednego. He ordered the furnace to be heated to a higher temperature, and the three were placed in it immediately. In this case God saved them, and the king was profoundly changed.

Shadrach, Meshach, and Abednego witnessed on the job. They stood their ground when it came to worship. They gave effective verbal and life-style witness and were able to influence their boss. They witnessed well at work.

Scripture and Personal Application

Colossians 4:2-6 says, "Devote yourselves to prayer, being watchful and thankful. And pray for us, too, that God may open a door for our message, so that we may proclaim the mystery of Christ, for which I am in chains. Pray that I may proclaim it clearly, as I should. Be wise in the way you act toward outsiders; make the most of every opportunity. Let your conversation be always full of grace, seasoned with salt, so that you may know how to answer everyone."

These few verses present three key ingredients relating to witnessing. First, prayer is important so that God will open up opportunities. We don't have to bang on doors or be overly aggressive. Second, our life-styles must reflect wisdom; outsiders are observing how we live. Third, our speech is important. In light of the last three verses, we can't be a witness without speaking—conversation, proclamation, clarity of expression, and responding to questions are all mentioned as being important. These can be summarized as "knock, walk, and talk." Be prepared to share your feelings or experiences regarding these three witnessing concepts.

____

____

____

The Great Commission, found in Matthew 28:16-20, says that we should go into the world and make disciples for Christ. Is the "world" for most of us where we work, or is it a far-off land? If we accept the Great Commission, in what ways can we allow it to influence our behavior in the marketplace?

Psalm 34:1 says, "I will extol the Lord at all times; his praise will always be on my lips." This doesn't sound like a bashful, reluctant witness!

On the other hand, Proverbs 25:11 says, "A word aptly spoken is like apples of gold in settings of silver." How does this relate to witnessing at work?

Peter exhorts us, "Always be prepared to give an answer to everyone who asks you to give the reason for the hope that you have. But do this with gentleness and respect, keeping a clear conscience, so that those who speak maliciously against your good behavior in Christ may be ashamed of their slander" (I Pet. 3:15, 16). Does this sound practical in today's marketplace? What experience have you had with trying to implement this passage?

"Be very careful, then, how you live—not as unwise but as wise, making the most of every opportunity, because the days are evil" (Eph. 5:15, 16). How do you make the most of witnessing opportunities at work? What things could you do to begin improving the quality of your witness?

"And they were all filled with the Holy Spirit and spoke the word of God boldly" (Acts 4:31b). Are there any drawbacks to having a bold personal witness at work? What are they? What is the role of the Holy Spirit in increasing our sensitivity to potential witnessing situations?

Does Proverbs 12:23 excuse us from our opportunities to witness at work, or anywhere else? Why or why not?

Discussion Questions

1. What are some of your personal experiences with witnessing at work? How do you witness? How effective do you believe you are?

2. What are a few of the techniques you can use to generate witnessing opportunities? Do you pray specifically for witnessing opportunities at work?

3. Based on your experience, what works and what doesn't work in terms of witnessing and leading people to Christ, particularly at work?

4. How does being an active Christian witness affect your "image," especially among customers and fellow workers? How much does that matter to you?

5. Have you tried any new and creative approaches in your personal witnessing? If so, share about them.

LESSON PLANS

This course on *Christianity in the Workplace* calls for a great deal of discussion and personal opinion. You will have no trouble filling up your group time by simply going through the discussion questions within each chapter. As leader of the group, however, you will want to make sure that participants move beyond an open-ended discussion into practical life response.

The following lesson plans are designed to help you do just that. Consider these activities as suggestions only. Use what you can, but feel free to skip portions or rearrange the order to fit your group's needs.

Important Notes

• Each week you may want to have group members commit to a specific action in response to the concepts you are discussing. These commitments can be written down on the back cover of this book, or on a separate sheet of paper. Keeping the response in mind each session will help you know what questions and activities to focus on and what can be skipped when time runs short.

• We generally do not recommend that you solicit answers by merely reading through the workbook item by item. Instead, you'll choose questions and other learning activities that help learners to use their homework assignments without parroting back the material item by item. On the other hand, when you do not cover workbook assignments systematically, give learners a chance to raise questions spurred by their homework, or to share discoveries that were particularly meaningful to them. Specific lesson plans won't always remind you to do this, yet learners may have pressing questions or exciting discoveries that you should incorporate into the sessions.

• Look through all of these lessons to note places where advance preparation is needed, or materials must be gotten well before the class session. That way you won't be caught off guard.

• Preceding Lesson 1, schedule an Introductory Meeting of your study group. Distribute the *Christianity in the Workplace* workbooks and introduce these distinctives of this course:

1. Much of the content in this course has been drawn from focus group sessions in which "real, live" working people discussed relevant issues pertaining to being a Christian at work. They raise many significant issues that don't always have easy answers.

2. Give a brief explanation of the dual authorship of this book. Their work represents a blending of a businessman's and a Bible scholar's perspective.

3. Have each group member share about his or her current occupation (you might want to limit this to what their job is, what they like most about it, and their greatest challenge to being a Christian on the job). If your group has over twelve members, share in small groups of five or six.

4. If desired, share some information on the Biblical basis for work. Consult the supplemental LAMP leader's guide (ordering information on page 8) for additional insights.

5. Stress the need for advanced preparation in order for this course to be most effective. Hand out the books and assign the first chapter for your next meeting.

• The cultivation of meaningful relationships among group members is integral to the success of this course. Incorporate key ingredients for healthy group life into each session: mutual accountability for application, personal sharing of struggles as well as victories on the job, and intercessory prayer.

Lesson 1

FOCUS: Give each group member a piece of paper and about five minutes to draw a candle divided into segments showing how they spend their time in a typical week. How much time is spent at work, at church, with family and friends, etc.? Let group members come up with their own divisions. Break into small groups to share candles. *Do any group members seem to be burning their candles at both ends?* Regather. **Ask:** What does this exercise teach us about priorities? What unique problems and opportunities do we have as Christians in setting priorities?

DISCOVER: Begin by asking for insights from the Scripture study portions of chapter one (*Snapshot from the Past* and *Scripture and Personal Application).*

• What verse(s) do you find particularly helpful in setting priorities? Why?
• How do I Corinthians 10:31 and Colossians 3:23, 24 apply to our work lives? In what specific ways have you been able to apply these verses in your work?
• Read Matthew 6:25-34. How seriously *do* you take your work? How seriously *should* you take it?

Point out that we are often prone to compartmentalize our lives into Christian and secular. For example, we do church work and regular work, we listen to Christian music and secular music, etc. What danger is there in doing this?

DISCUSS: The following questions do not directly parallel the *Discussion Questions* in chapter one. If one of the following questions relates to a question from the chapter, then a reference to that number is given in parentheses. Pick and choose from among all the questions to move your discussion toward a specific, life-changing response.

1. What is your biggest problem in setting and keeping your priorities? (Q. 1)
2. Why do Christians sometimes resent being "overcommitted" to the church more often than they resent being "overcommitted" to their jobs? (Q. 3)
3. What tips can you offer others who have difficulty with priorities? (Q. 2) What works for you?

RESPOND: Have group members write down *one* specific personal commitment about their priorities. For example, one person might commit to getting home by 6:00 pm each evening. Another might commit to spending a half hour in quiet time with the Lord before work each day. These commitments can be written on the inside of the back cover of this book or on a separate sheet of paper to be added to each week.

Break into groups of two or three to share these commitments and pray about them.

Lesson 2

FOCUS: Break into "companies" of three or four employees each. Announce that each company is to meet for five minutes to determine a company name and to decide what product or service they will offer. They must be prepared to present their idea to "The Board of Directors" who will award one grant of $100,000 to the company with the most workable idea. Give groups some paper and markers to come up with necessary visuals.

After five minutes are up, gather all groups and have each company make a short presentation to the others.

Vote on the winning presentation.

Ask: What did this exercise teach you about decision making? What decisions did you have to make? How did you make them? What types of decisions are most difficult for you to make where you work?

DISCOVER: Make a list on the chalkboard or a large sheet of paper of all the advantages Christians have in making decisions. Encourage group members to refer to their answers throughout chapter two for ideas.

- What does the parable of the talents (Matt. 25:14-30) teach us about decision making? What role does risk play in making decisions?
- What insights into decision making did you gain from the first two chapters of I Corinthians?

DISCUSS: Make another list of practical tips group members can offer for making difficult decisions at work.

1. Give examples of how prayer and the Holy Spirit have helped you make decisions. (Q. 3)
2. How do you know if and when you have made a good decision? (Q. 4) How do you judge past decisions?
3. Pair up and share one major decision you had to make at work in the past, how you made it, and if you know now whether it was the right or wrong decision.
4. What tips or suggestions would you offer others for making better decisions?

RESPOND: Ask group members to write down (on the inside back page cover or the separate sheet of paper used last session) one major decision they are facing at work right now, or with regard to their career future. Then write one specific principle from this session that can be applied to help make that decision.

Close with a time of group sharing and prayer, focusing on major decisions people need to make this week.

Lesson 3

FOCUS: Pass out copies of old magazines and have group members clip advertisements from companies of products they consider excellent. Do the same for companies/products that they *don't* consider excellent.

After a few minutes of hunting, share your findings (perhaps by making two large collages) and list names of companies and products on the board under the headings, "Excellent" and "Not Excellent." **Ask:** What things contribute to making these products/companies excellent or not excellent?

DISCOVER:
Allow for a time of silence while participants review their findings from the Scripture portions of chapter 3. Based on this review, have them share their answers to this question: How does God define excellence?

DISCUSS:
1. What potential conflicts are there between a company's definition of excellence and your personal definition of excellence as a Christian? In what ways are the two definitions compatible?
2. What should our motive be for being excellent on the job? What dangers do we face if we seek after excellence for the wrong motives? Give examples from personal experience.
3. What role does competition play in business? (Q. 3) Is business competition compatible with your Christian value system? When, if ever, do your values conflict with commonly accepted competitive business practices?
4. When is/isn't it appropriate for a Christian to "toot his or her horn" on the job?

RESPOND: Encourage group members to complete this sentence: One way I can be more excellent in my work is to ____

in order to ____.
(This response can be drawn, in part, from individual responses to discussion question 1 within chapter 3.)

Share as appropriate in small groups or one to one. Close with a time of prayer, focusing on the excellence of God.

Lesson 4

FOCUS: Two sessions ago we looked at decision making on the job. In this lesson we will look at planning. In some ways these two concepts overlap; however, planning focuses on a longer-term time frame.

Break into groups of four or five. This time, instead of forming companies, announce that each group is a family. Give each family five minutes to plan a vacation. Go!

Gather together to discuss this activity:

- How did you go about your planning? (Many groups probably started by determining who they are, where they want to go, and how and when they can get there.)
- What is the purpose of planning?
- Is it possible to plan too much? Support your answer.

DISCOVER:

- What characteristics of Nehemiah impressed you the most?
- How do you reconcile James 4:13-17 with current corporate planning practices and other Scripture verses in this chapter?
- Read Proverbs 21:30. How do you know if a plan is "against the Lord?" Share your experiences in this area as recorded in the book.
- What excuses might we be tempted to give for not planning (based on Romans 8:28 and other verses)?

DISCUSS: Draw a straight line continuum from one end of the board or large sheet of paper to the other. Label one end "Flow with the Spirit" and the other end "Formal planning for everything." Give each group member an opportunity to mark at what point on the continuum they are most comfortable operating in their work.

DISCUSS:
1. How does being a Christian influence your planning? (Q. 2) What difference does it make?
2. What difficulties do you face in your planning?
3. What part does the Lord play in your planning and what is your responsibility?

RESPOND: Choose one Scripture verse from this chapter (possibly from Proverbs) to memorize. How will that verse assist your planning? As a group, have each person share what verse they chose and how it might assist them.

Share together some of the major business plans of various individuals in your group. Pray for vision and guidance to know that your plans are God's plans.

Lesson 5

FOCUS: Divide into two groups. Have one group list all the characteristics of "the perfect boss" and let the other group come up with characteristics of "the perfect employee." After a few minutes, have one member of each group write their group's list on the board or a large sheet of paper. Now compare the lists.

- In what ways are the lists similar? Different?
- What difference does being a Christian make in being a supervisor? Employee?

DISCOVER: Since many different aspects of the employee/supervisor relationship are explored in chapter five, you might want to focus in on the idea of being a servant.

- From your personal study, what are some of the Bible's requirements for being a good boss? Employee?

• In what ways can a boss also be a servant?
• In what ways does the Biblical model of service conflict with common notions about being a good boss/employee?
• How can an employee serve a boss who is very difficult to work for?

DISCUSS: Read the first two paragraphs of *Snapshots from the Present.*

1. How would you respond to the person who made these comments? What has your experience been?
2. Should we have higher expectations of a Christian employee or employer? (Q. 4) Support your answer.
3. How much of yourself should you reveal on the job? Do people at work know you are a Christian? If so, what difference does this make? If not, why? (Q. 2)
4. When is it most difficult for you to be a servant at work?

RESPOND: Go back to your lists of the perfect employer and employee. How compatible are these traits with the notion of Christian service? If you are a supervisor, choose one characteristic from "the perfect boss" list that you need to improve. Those who are employees should do the same from the other list. Some people should choose a characteristic from each list. Give group members a few moments to write these down and then break into small groups to share responses and pray.

Lesson 6

FOCUS: Make sure your introductory remarks include those who are married and those who aren't. We all need to understand the unique stresses that dual-income families face. Depending on the composition of your group, you might want to expand this lesson to include the needs of single parents and unmarried singles as well.

Option 1: Ahead of time, invite two or three working women to be on a panel. Have group members ask them questions like "What is the most difficult part of balancing home and career?"; "For what reasons do you work?" "Where do you get the support you need?"

Option 2: If your class is composed of many working couples, select two to four couples and have all the husbands leave the room while you ask the wives two or three questions (lighthearted or serious). Write down their answers. Have husbands come in and see if they can match their wives' responses (ala *The Newlywed Game*). Sample questions: What percent of the housework does the man do? Would the husband be bothered if the wife made more money than himself? What is the biggest source of tension from both working? Whose job do you talk about most?

DISCOVER: In small groups, discuss Proverbs 31:10-31. What evidence is there that this woman was a "working" woman? Have each group pen a few extra verses in the style of this proverb to describe a husband of noble character. Let each group share their creations.

- Regather and share responses to the comments on Ecclesiastes 4:9-12 relating to spouses working.

Discuss: Don't get hung up on a lengthy discussion of whether women should work outside the home. That is not the goal of this lesson. Rather, you should focus your attention on ways of supporting those who do.

1. Let's make a list of all the stress points that come from situations where both spouses work. (Q. 1)
2. How do couples deal with these stresses? (Q. 2, 3)
3. What is your church doing, or could it do, to provide support to working couples? (Q. 5)

RESPOND: Direct group members in this activity: If you are in a situation where husband and wife work, list one major stress point and a new idea you have for dealing with it based on today's discussion. If you are not currently in a dual-income situation, list one specific way you could support a working couple that you know.

Share related concerns together and close in a time of conversational prayer.

Lesson 7

Focus: Ask for two volunteers or select two outgoing individuals. Have them "swap occupations" then interview each one with questions like: "Describe your typical day"; "What's the hardest part about your job?"; "What qualities should an individual possess in order to do well at your job?" Encourage them to give humorous responses if they so desire. If time permits, do the same thing with another pair.

• What are some of the difficulties associated with changing jobs or careers? Encourage those who have changed jobs to share from their personal experience.

Discover: Talk through the three principles for approaching a job change from Marlowe Embree (page 64) on the board or a large sheet of paper.

1. Servanthood—needs
2. Stewardship—gifts
3. Calling—needs + gifts

Have group members apply this model to their own career plans. How is this model helpful? What else would you add to it?

• Read Ecclesiastes 3:9-13. In general, are workers today too restless? Support your answer.
• Comment on Proverbs 23:4 in light of people's attempts to climb the career ladder. What motives are driving your career decisions?

Discuss:
1. How does being a Christian influence your career choice? (Q. 3)
2. Draw a continuum on the board or a large sheet of paper. Label one end "Extremely Satisfied" and the other "Extremely Dissatisfied." Have each group member put an "x" on the line (or above it) to indicate how they are feeling about where they are in respect to their career at this time. Discuss what factors lead to contentment and what factors lead to dissatisfaction. (Q. 5) What guidelines should we use to evaluate our career progress?
3. What special concerns do those currently retired or approaching retirement have?

Respond: How likely are you to get a promotion, or make a job or career change in the next 12 months? (Very likely. Somewhat likely. Not very likely.) If very or somewhat likely, what is one thing you need to do to prepare for that change? If not very likely, how can you help a friend who is in the midst of a job transition?

Share responses and pray for one another.

Lesson 8

Focus: Read the following four questions and have group members write their responses:

1. You've just been told that you lost your job. Write down one word to describe how you feel.
2. You've now been out of work for some time. Write down one or two words to describe how you feel about yourself. How do you feel about being with other people? How do you feel toward God?

Share responses. At this point you may want to have someone who is currently unemployed or recently unemployed share his or her responses to these and other questions.

Discover:
• How does the quote from *Forbes* magazine (page 67) make you feel?
• What can we learn from the life of Joseph to help us through and/or prepare for times of unemployment?
• What other Scriptural insight into unemployment did you gain from your individual study?

Discuss:
1. What special resources are available to us as Christians to help us deal with unemployment? (Q. 1 and 2)
2. What specific things would you do tomorrow if you became unemployed today?
3. Why is our employment so tied up with our self esteem?

Respond: If you are currently working, what is one specific thing you can do to prepare yourself for potential unemployment? (Q. 3) If you are currently out of work, what is one lesson you've learned that you would want others to know? Share responses in small groups and pray for work-related concerns.

Lesson 9

Focus: Break into groups of three or four and have each group create an advertisement that a business might use to exploit the fact that they are "Christian." Encourage the use of exaggeration. These ads can be done on paper or scripted out as if for radio or television. Some examples: Christian toothpaste, used cars for Christians, Christian garbage collecting service.

After sharing your creations, ask:
• Have you ever seen individuals or organizations exploiting their Christianity for profit? Share examples.
• When does/doesn't it matter to you to deal with other Christians in business?

DISCOVER:
• What are the pros and cons of dealing with other Christians in business? List these on the board as individuals share both positive and negative experiences.
• Read II Corinthians 6:14-16 in light of Christians working together in business partnerships. Do these verses apply to this situation, or not?
• How might Galatians 6:1-8 apply to doing business with other Christians?

DISCUSS:
1. What issues did this chapter raise in your mind?
2. How do you feel about using church members as sales prospects? (Q. 2)
3. Should Christians go out of their way to patronize businesses or employ other believers? (Q. 3)
4. How do you feel goods and services from "Christian companies" compare to other companies? (Q. 4) Is there such a thing as a Christian company?

RESPOND: Think of one letter you would write to either an individual Christian or a Christian organization to encourage them *or* gently rebuke them. Briefly describe what you might say. Whether you actually write this letter is up to you! (Example: perhaps someone recently received a catalog for Christian clothing that used Scripture verses out of context and seemed to exploit believers. What kind of letter might be written to the company attempting to sell this merchandise?)

Share in smaller groups as appropriate. Close in a time of group prayer thanking God for one another.

Lesson 10

FOCUS: This chapter raises so many issues that you might want to consider covering it in two weeks (especially if one of the other lessons in this book seems less relevant to your particular group).

Start with a few words about the difference between ethics and honesty. Point out that you will not be dealing with black and white issues like cheating on expense accounts, but on "gray" issues.

Give everyone an opportunity to write down an ethical business dilemma in a way that it has to be answered with a yes or a no. For example, "You walk into your boss' office to put something on her desk and can't help but see her paycheck. She isn't there at the moment. Do you look at the amount?" Jot down some reasons for your answer.

Collect the questions and read one to the group. Let each group member vote yes or no (preferably in writing). Tally the responses and move on to another question. Do as many as you have time for.

DISCOVER: Begin by listing some of the major ethical lapses that have been in the news lately concerning government, religious, and business leaders. Why do we seem to be hearing such stories more often?

- What made Old Testament Daniel an ethical person?
- What does the Bible say about ethics in business? Have each group member summarize in one or two sentences (based on their personal study of the Scripture passages).

DISCUSS:

1. Make a list of the most prevalent ethical business issues facing your group members. Can you find Scripture verses that apply to each issue? (Q. 1) What issues are more a matter of honesty than of ethics?

2. Should Christians have higher ethical standards than others? In general, do they? Share examples.

3. How can you evaluate another person's ethical standards? (Q. 2) Is this being judgmental?

RESPOND: Have each person list one common business practice he or she engages in that may be unethical, or one way to increase his or her sensitivity to ethical issues. If individuals are able to think of possible unethical practices, encourage them to pray for wisdom concerning that practice. Share responses in small groups and close in prayer.

Lesson 11

FOCUS: Pass out hymnbooks to group members. Have them look through various hymns that have to do with fellowship and call out any benefits of fellowship that they can find there. See how many you can come up with in five minutes. As an option, break into teams and see which team comes up with the most benefits as found in the hymn lyrics.

List these benefits on the board and ask for others.

• How important is it to you to have Christian fellowship on the job? Allow various members to share their personal experiences.

DISCOVER: Now list some of the problems of having fellowship on the job. Perhaps these problems are obstacles to having fellowship, or negative consequences from having too much fellowship.

• What does Hebrews 3:13 mean in a work setting? What specific ways have you encouraged other Christians at work?
• What other Scriptural insights do group members have from their personal study?

DISCUSS:
1. Suppose all Christian fellowship outside the church building and homes was suddenly outlawed. How would you cope?
2. Some people say that work is not the place for fellowship. How do you respond to such a notion? (Q. 4)
3. Have you ever had a period in your life where you lacked fellowship? Describe your experience.

4. Give some practical suggestions to a new employee who is actively seeking fellowship at work. (Q. 5)

RESPOND: Give group members an opportunity to rate their level of fellowship at work (Too much, Not enough, About right.)

As you close in prayer, concentrate on thanking God for the many benefits of Christian fellowship that were listed at the beginning of your session.

Lesson 12

FOCUS: Start this session with different pairs of individuals roleplaying the following situations:

1. An overly aggressive person witnessing on the job;
2. An overly timid person avoiding any opportunity to witness at work;
3. A Christian being a bad witness at work.

Then ask the following questions:

- What is a witness?
- Why do so many of us have difficulty witnessing, especially at work?

DISCOVER: Summarize the three key ingredients relating to witnessing found in Colossians 4:2-6:

1. Pray for opportunities and God will open doors (knock).
2. Our life-styles must reflect wisdom (walk).
3. Our speech is important (talk).

- Share examples of how you have seen these concepts at work in witnessing to others.
- What kinds of prayers have you prayed for God to open doors? What keeps us from praying this type of prayer more often?
- What does it mean to make the most of every opportunity? Give some examples of opportunities you have either seized or not seized and then regretted later.

• What does it mean to "Let your conversation be full of grace, seasoned with salt (vs. 6)?" Give examples.
• How would you answer someone who asks:
Why are you different from the rest? What makes you so happy? You're a Christian aren't you? I want whatever it is you've got.
• Apply I Peter 3:15, 16 to witnessing at work.

DISCUSS:
1. What tips would you offer others for effective ways to witness to others at work? (Q. 1-3, 5)
2. What difficulties do you encounter in witnessing to others at work?
3. Would you say you tend to be on the timid side or the aggressive side in your witness at work? At what point does one become too aggressive? Too timid?

RESPOND: Challenge each person to write down the name of one individual (at work or elsewhere) that they would like an opportunity to talk with about Jesus. Then have each person check one of the areas (knock, walk, or talk) that they feel is in most need of improvement in their own witness. Share in small groups or one to one.

If time permits, wrap up this course with a brief review. Ask for volunteers to share one specific way they have benefited from this study. Encourage everyone to look through their commitments and to follow through on them.

Close in a time of prayer. You might want to consider having group members simply call out the name of the individual with whom they would like an opportunity to witness. Then expect God to open doors!